MW01223966

MAKE INSTAGRAM WORK FOR YOUR BUSINESS

The complete guide
to marketing your business,
generating leads, finding
new customers and building
your brand on Instagram

Alex Stearn

ISBN-13:978-1502911094
ISBN-10:1502911094

This book is dedicated
to Sonia, Tony and Ollie.

Any Questions?

Thank you for your recent purchase of 'Make Instagram Work for your Business' I really hope you will enjoy the book and your business will benefit greatly.

If you have any questions about the book or about social media marketing in general, please do not hesitate to contact me by email at alex@alexstearn.com or on **Facebook at** www.Facebook.com/alexandrastearn and I will do my best to reply as soon as possible. I also offer regular updates, ebooks and social media tips in my newsletter at www.alexstearn.com and a group on Facebook which is all about supporting each other in our social media efforts and networking. Would love you to join us at this link

http://bit.ly/yourgroup

Looking forward to connecting

Table of Contents

Chapter Nine

Chapter Ten

Chapter Eleven

Chapter Twelve

WHY THIS BOOK?

SO YOU WANT to launch a Instagram marketing campaign for your business or maybe you've already done so and you're just not achieving the results you expected. Perhaps that's because you've found it difficult to build a sizeable following or your audience is simply not converting into paying customers.

Every day hundreds of businesses are setting out on their social media journey excited about the opportunities and possibilities that this relatively new type of marketing may be able to offer their business. Some are getting it right, reaping huge rewards, and managing to leverage the enormous power of the Internet through social media, but the majority are struggling to make it work at all. Those who are struggling often don't really understand exactly how social media works and launch into a campaign without any plan or strategy or without even knowing exactly what they are looking to achieve. They perhaps create a Instagram page and ask their web developer to add a 'like' or 'follow' button to their website, invite their friends and customers to join their page, and then start posting updates. After a while they realize that whatever they are doing is having little or no positive effect on their sales and they are left with the same questions:

- How do I leverage the almighty power of the Internet and Instagram to make money for my business?
- How do I find the people who are interested in my products?
- How do I draw these people away from Instagram and onto my website or blog?
- And the ultimate question, how do I convert all these people into

paying customers and actually profit from Instagram marketing?

These businesses either continue to go round in circles waiting for a miracle to happen, give up altogether, or continue to believe that there is a way they can make social media work for their business and start looking for a solution to solve their problem.

This is exactly what I did and this is where my social media journey began. I started to look for a solution but kept coming up with the same brick walls, the same fluffy vague information about engagement, and lots of very expensive courses. I read books and blogs but they never really seemed to solve my problem and get to the heart of the matter.

I then decided to make it my mission to demystify the hype surrounding social media marketing and discover everything I possibly could about how to make all the major social media platforms work for any business. I studied literally hundreds of campaigns to see what was working and what wasn't and completely immersed myself in social media marketing until all my questions were answered. My aim was to discover how to utilize the almighty power of Instagram to help any business achieve their marketing goals. I made it my mission to leave no stone unturned in terms of a marketing opportunity which could help any business generate leads and ultimately increase their sales.

After 18 months of immersing myself in this subject, I am now delighted to hand this information over to you. My goal is to help you save your time and your resources and provide you with a highly effective system to make Instagram work for your business. In this book I am going to share with you everything you need to know to take your business to the next level and leverage the power of Instagram so you can achieve the highest profits, the best customers, the best ambassadors for your business, and make money 24/7.

This book is perfect for anyone who is seriously committed to growing their business and achieving incredible results. Whether you are just starting out or already up and running and uncertain how to make Instagram work for your business then this book is to going to teach you exactly how to do just that. You will have absolutely everything you need to learn, prepare, plan, and implement a campaign which is going to help you generate leads and find new customers.

The fact is, Instagram, and social media as a whole, is a game changer, a dream come true for any business and has completely revolutionized the way business is being done today. However, it is still just a marketing tool and while on the face of it seems free, if not used correctly and effectively, it is simply just a waste of your time and resources.

In this book you will not only learn the skills and strategies of Instagram marketing but also everything you need to know about how social media works in marketing and how to plan, prepare, and execute your campaign including:

- What social media marketing is, why it is so good, why it is absolutely essential for any business today, and why so many businesses are getting it wrong
- The psychology behind why people make buying decisions and how you can use this knowledge to succeed in your Instagram campaign and other social media campaigns as well
- The importance of defining your business, your brand, and your target audience and how to do this
- How to set clear goals and objectives for your social media campaign
- How to prepare your website or blog for success, capture leads, and build a highly targeted list of subscribers
- How to plan, create, maintain, and manage your Instagram campaign
- Detailed information about how to set up your business profile

on Instagram
- The strategies you need to implement to attract the best prospects and build and maintain a targeted following on Instagram and build lasting relationships
- The importance of content and how to easily find ideas to create content for your page
- How to convert your followers into leads, paying customers, and ambassadors and brand advocates of your business
- How to constantly measure and monitor your campaign so you can steer your campaign to achieve your goals

A great deal of love and joy has gone into writing this book. Love of the subject itself and joy at the opportunity to share with you the information and knowledge within. I have devoted 18 months to researching and writing this book, along with the others in the series, in order to uncover the truth about social media. I truly hope you will be inspired and that your business will thrive and flourish by implementing the suggested strategies.

As mentioned above there are books available on Kindle and in paperback for each of the major social media platforms including Facebook, Twitter , LinkedIn, Google + YouTube, Pinterest and Tumblr. The big book, 'Make Social Media Work for your Business' covers includes all
8 books. If you are planning on buying more than a few books then I would suggest purchasing this book rather than each individual book. The big book 'Make Social Media Work for your Business' is available from $9.99 at this Link

Even within the time it has taken to write this book, certain things have changed in the social media world and so some sections have been updated to reflect those changes. The world of social media is dynamic and therefore it is my commitment to keep updating this book as and when those changes occur. If you wish to keep up-to-date with latest social media updates, tips, and changes, please subscribe to my newsletter at www.alexstearn.com

CHAPTER ONE

THE IMPORTANCE OF UNDERSTANDING SOCIAL MEDIA MARKETING

BEFORE LAUNCHING INTO your Instagram marketing campaign, and so that you are absolutely committed when you do start, you will need to be convinced that social media marketing does actually work for businesses and that you are going to be able to make it work for yours. In this chapter, you will learn why social media marketing has gained so much attention, why so many brands are using it, and why it is so different from other forms of marketing. The aim here is to help you truly appreciate the power and importance of this relatively new method of marketing. Once you are totally convinced that the time you will be investing will be truly worthwhile, you will be ready to launch into your Instagram marketing campaign with strength, confidence, and conviction.

So what is social media exactly? Social media is the place where people connect with other people using the technology we have today. It's where people engage, share, cooperate, interact, learn, enjoy, and build relationships. The number of ways in which we connect with each other has grown massively in recent years from telephone, mobiles, email, text, video, newspaper, or radio to what we have today, the social media networks.

As humans, the majority of us want to belong, be accepted, loved, respected, and heard. We are social animals and social media has provided us with new tools which allow us to be more social, even if our lives are more hectic and we are living a long way from our friends and family. It's now not unusual for family and friends to be located at opposite sides of the country or even in a different country. Our lives have become far busier and more transient than ever, and yet we still crave the same social connections as we did 100 years ago when we would probably have been living in the same village or town as our family and friends.

The impact that social media is having on our lives and on businesses is massive. Social media has completely changed the way we communicate and the way we do everything. It has made connecting with people and building relationships so much easier. Now, staying in contact with someone we may only have met once is straightforward. We can find old friends we went to school or college with, and the opportunities for making new contacts are limitless. Social media has given us the ability to quickly and easily share ideas, experiences, and information on anything we like, and we can find out about anyone, any business, or anything. With the massive growth in smartphone ownership, most people can now access the internet instantly. We are living in a virtual world and we can literally connect to anyone, from anywhere, at anytime.

Understanding the reasons why people love social media so much will help give you a really good idea about how, as a business, you need to engage so you can connect with your audience and grow and maintain that audience. Most people are on social media to be social, to connect with other family and friends, and to have fun. However, here are a few more reasons why so many use and love social media:

To be part of a community or common interest group
To express their feelings and have a voice
To reconnect with old college or school friends
To find out where their friends are
To tell their friends where they are
To announce a piece of news
To find out if a product or service is good

To connect with thought leaders

To make business contacts

To follow brands

To keep up-to-date with current affairs, football scores

To connect with famous people

To find inspiration and motivation

To learn by reading blogs, watching videos, and listening to podcasts

To help other people

To launch a business

To advertise and grow a business

To make new friends

To make new contacts

To connect with others in different countries

To make a difference

To be entertained

To communicate quickly and save time

To support important causes or people

To find a job

The power and enormity of social media

Everyone is doing Social! Okay, so not everyone is doing social media, but the majority of people are! Wherever you go you will see somebody with their heads down looking at some device, and you can bet your bottom dollar that they are accessing some social site, whether it's Instagram, Twitter, Instagram, LinkedIn, YouTube, Google+, Pinterest, or Snapchat.

The growth in social media is huge, and it's no wonder that it is being called 'The Social Media Revolution.' Without going into too much statistical information, it's safe to say that your customer is probably using at least one social network, either for personal or business use, and very likely to be accessing multiple sites.

All the social media platforms are growing at incredible speeds. You only have to type 'Social media statistics' into Google and you will blown away by the millions and billions. Instagram now has over one billion users and 95% of those users access it at least once a day and some more than five times. More than one billion unique users visit YouTube per month, and Twitter has 215 monthly active users. The most popular websites are social. The world loves social.

WHAT IS SOCIAL MEDIA MARKETING

Not long ago promoting a business could feel very much like being alone on a desert island. You could have a great idea but unless you had vast sums of money for television, magazine, or direct mail advertising then, frustratingly, your idea was very likely to remain a secret. Today it is totally different and social media has given businesses endless opportunities to reach their target audience, connect with new prospects, and enter new markets. The playing field has been levelled out, and now anyone with the right knowledge has more chance than ever of making their business a success.

Social media marketing is a relatively new form of marketing and refers to the processes, strategies, and tactics used by businesses on social networking sites and blogs to gain attention and ultimately increase their revenue. Businesses and large brands are now using the fact that people love to engage and connect with other people with the other very important fact that they are very likely to find their target audience on social media so that they can do the following:

- Find, reach, and connect with potential customers
- Drive traffic to a website or blog
- Stay connected and communicate with existing customers. It is a well-known fact that existing customers are far more likely to purchase and also pay more for a product than someone who has not bought before.
- To build trust, interest, and loyalty by interacting with your followers (potential customers) so that ultimately they will

purchase your product, continue to purchase your product, and hopefully recommend your product to their friends

- To produce content that users will share with their social network or recommend to their friends. Social media marketing strongly centers around the creation of content for a particular audience with the intention that it can be shared, 'liked', and commented on by the user. When this happens, the content is being passed to other users by word-of-mouth, the most powerful form of advertising.
- To listen and find out what your customers want

THE BIG LINK, THE PSYCHOLOGY BEHIND BUYING BEHAVIOUR

Not only have successful marketeers recognized that people want to engage with people, they have also tapped into the psychology behind why people make buying decisions and incorporated this into their social media campaigns.

As a business you will need to understand a great deal about your customers in order to market your products successfully to your target audience. Understanding how and why people make the final purchase decision will go a long way to help you discern how to make social media marketing actually work for your business. There seem to be a number of common factors that influence consumers when they are making their buying decision. Leveraging and using this knowledge with your Instagram campaign will be incredibly powerful and a recipe for success.

The 'like' factor

This is a biggie. When we look at the findings and the psychology behind buying decisions it often comes down to simply being likeable. Consumers are far more likely to buy a product from someone they like, respect, or trust. Word-of-mouth advertising has always proven to be the most powerful form of advertising and now Instagram has taken this to another level and managed to harness this online with the 'like' button. Having your business name or brand reach hundreds or even thousands of people is now possible, and someone only has to 'like' or interact with your business on social media and you can almost guarantee that someone else will see that interaction. The truth is people do business with people they like and are more likely to spread the word to their network about deals and special offers from people they like, trust, and respect.

Social proof

When a consumer finds themselves at a point of indecision they will look for social proof and seek advice and corroboration from others. They are far more likely to buy if they see that their friends or a similar group of people have bought or used product. People generally look to others for advice or look to see what others are buying to get over their personal insecurity when making a buying decision. This is why you see so many women shopping in pairs. The opinion of a friend about an item can often be the deciding factor when making the decision to buy or not.

Authority and reviews

Even before the Internet was introduced, people were keen to find reviews about products they were interested in buying, particularly if they were planning to make a major purchase. They would either buy a special magazine or seek information from an authoritative figure on a TV advertisement. Today, however, shoppers are far more savvy. They can smell an advert a mile off and they will go out of their way to find honest reviews about something they may want to buy. They are also spoilt for choice, not only with the number of products available to them but the fact that they can find a review about literally anything just by a simple search on the Internet or looking at a brand's Instagram account or Facebook Page. People always have and always will want as much evidence as possible that they are making the right buying decision. Any business who wants to succeed today needs to embrace this fact and try and gain as many reviews for their products and services as possible.

Reviews could be in the form of customer blog articles, reviews on your website, on social media sites, or articles in newspapers and magazines. Displaying articles, client testimonials, or the logos of magazines that you have been featured in on your website will also go a long way to building authority and gaining the trust of your prospects.

Scarcity or exclusivity

Scarcity or exclusivity can play a big part in people's buying decisions, and Instagram is a perfect place to communicate and use this factor to sell your products. If a product is scarce or less available, the consumer will often perceive that this product has greater value. As they become less available, the consumer fears that they may lose out on a great deal or a one-time offer. Giving your prospects a deadline or a specific time to purchase something or redeem an offer is an incredibly powerful way of focusing their mind to make a decision. When they know they need to make that decision by a certain time or they may lose out on a one-time deal, they are far more likely to make that decision. Another very effective way of using this factor is by simply suggesting to your prospects that by signing up for your email opt-in, they will be the first to hear about your new products or your exclusive offers.

Loyalty

Consumers do not like taking risks and often prefer to repeat their past purchasing behavior by buying from a brand they have bought from before. The majority of shoppers are brand loyal and social media is another way of nurturing this type of behavior by building up even deeper relationships with your customers through constant contact and updates.

Reciprocation

Reciprocation is a very powerful factor to take into consideration if you are looking to succeed on Instagram. As humans, the majority of us have a natural desire to repay favors and with Instagram you can really put this into practice. If you show support by either 'liking', sharing, or commenting on other people's content, not only will it attract their attention, they will, more often than not, return the favor by 'liking', commenting, and sharing your content. Also, if you are sharing great content on your network or offering good, valuable, and free advice, you are very likely to earn a great deal of respect. This will often result in a good payback of some sort later.

WHY IS SOCIAL MEDIA MARKETING SO GOOD FOR YOUR BUSINESS?

We know that an enormous number of people are accessing the social networks to connect with each other, and now we need to understand why this type of marketing is so different from other forms of marketing and why it is so important for your business. The main reason is that social media marketing is fundamentally more effective. Consumers today are smart. They are tired and suspicious of traditional forms of advertising. More often than not they will fast forward a TV commercial, switch channels, or skip a printed page with an advertisement on it. Today's consumers want to hear that a product has been tried and tested. They want to see a product being demonstrated, and they often need a recommendation from a trusted source, most likely a fried, to make a purchase. Here are some reasons why social media marketing is more effective than other, more traditional, marketing methods:

Social media offers you the opportunity to find the right target audience.
Never before has it been so easy to find and access your target audience. With the information that most of the social networks hold about their users, you can now target and find the very people who are more likely to buy your products or services.

Social media allows you to have direct contact with your customer.
You literally have the opportunity to communicate directly and stay in touch with your customer, unlike traditional forms of advertising. For

instance with a Facebook business page or a 'places' page, you can stay in touch with your customers well after they have left your establishment or bought your product. You can also send them offers to encourage them to return or buy your product again.

Social media marketing harnesses the power of peer recommendation.

The majority of people trust recommendations by others. Social media marketing is the only media that can harness the most powerful form of advertising, word of mouth, by making it possible for consumers to communicate with each other and vote for products or services by pressing the 'like' or 'follow' button.

Social media helps builds your brand.

Never has there been so much opportunity to build your brand. Your brand is simply the most valuable asset of your business. Your brand is what differentiates you from other businesses. It is the image people have of your business, and it establishes loyalty. With social media you have the opportunity to engage with consumers and build positive brand associations in a way that no other media can. Consumers now have the choice and opportunity to follow your brand. If they do, this means they actually want to hear or see what you have to say.

Social media humanizes your brand.

Social media allows you to communicate with your audience in a totally unique way. Your brand is no longer a rigid logo but a personality. Not only can you show your appreciation and the value you place on your audience, but they can also grow to love your brand too. No other type of marketing allows this type of two-way live communication.

Offers continual exposure to your product.

Social media marketing allows you to be continually in contact with your followers. Once you build your audience, they can hear from you and see your brand on a daily basis. Statistics prove that, on average, a person needs to see or connect with a brand seven times before purchasing. This is a difficult and costly goal to achieve with traditional forms of advertising but incredibly easy with social media marketing.

The consumer has a choice.

Unlike other traditional methods of advertising, the consumer has the opportunity to be exposed to your product by choice. They can opt in or out whenever they want.

Your audience is relaxed and receptive.

The majority of people are accessing Instagram and other social media accounts in their own leisure time to be social. Social media is all about connecting with friends and relatives, meeting new people and making new contacts. People are far more receptive to hearing from a brand in their own time when they are relaxed, as long as the brand is offering some kind of value and is not continually pushing their product.

You can continually engage with your audience.

Social media marketing allows businesses to have an ongoing dialogue with their audience like no other media. Fans or followers who have interacted with a business on social media are far more likely to visit their online store than those who did not.

It's viral.

Once your followers choose to interact or share your content then this interaction is seen by their network of friends who are then also exposed to your brand. This is how viral growth happens, which results in audience growth and brand awareness, more prospects, more customers, and increased sales.

Social media is an asset to your business.

Unlike other forms of advertising where you see your marketing investment disappear, your Instagram account, or any other social media account, becomes a valuable asset. If you are using your social media marketing correctly, your network will grow, you will be building trust, and your asset will increase in value. With traditional advertising, once an advert is delivered the connection with the buyer is over and you see your investment literally disappear.

It is like having your own broadcasting channel.

Once you have your campaign set up and your follower numbers are growing, you literally have your very own broadcasting channel which you own. You can communicate with your followers about anything 24/7. Nobody can take this away unless, of course, you are not running it correctly and you are losing followers. If you provide content that is so useful and interesting, your followers will keep coming back again and again to check if you have anything new to say. You then have a following of people who will associate your valuable content and their positive experience with your brand.

You can offer your customers proof of trading.

Having a social media presence that is active and engaging helps reassure customers that your business actually exists. They can easily check, by comments left by customers, whether your business is reputable and trustworthy. They are far more likely to buy from you once they see your active presence on social media.

Social media improves your search engine ranking.

Google counts social sharing when ranking your website or blog. If people are finding your content valuable then the search engines will register this and rank your site accordingly. Social media sites are highly ranked in the search engines and having a well-optimized profile is yet another way of being found on the Internet.

Social media opens up a worldwide playing field.

It used to be only the large companies who could afford to build their brand and have the opportunity to access thousands of potential customers. Now everybody with a business has the opportunity to reach thousands of people, both nationally and globally, grow their business, and benefit from one of the most powerful forms of marketing. Having a business no longer needs be a lonely island. You literally have the opportunity to get your message heard by thousands of people through social networking.

Social media provides advantages for the consumer.
With just a few clicks of the mouse or the tap of a smartphone, consumers can be in contact with any business very quickly. For the first time they have a very powerful voice. Their opinions are taken seriously. They are and valued whether they are in contact through customer service or just following a brand because they are interested. People want to remain close to the brands they are interested in, and this is shown by the continual rise in the number of people following brands.

You can listen to your customers.
You can now hear what your customers are saying about your product or service, and you can use this information to improve or develop your products and customer service. This helps your business become more transparent and shows your customers that you care and value their opinion, which ultimately leads to more trust for your brand.

You can become a thought leader.
By producing valuable and rich content for your audience, you can become a thought leader. Not only will this help if you are a personal brand, but it will also help build trust and reputation for any business or brand.

You can make a difference.
With social media you can actually make a positive difference in people's lives. Once you know your audience, you can provide content which is of value to them and will actually help them in some way. Helping your audience like this goes a long way in helping them remember your business when they are ready to make that purchasing decision.

It promotes endless opportunities.

Never has there been so much opportunity to have direct access to so many people, and neither has there been so much opportunity for any business of any size to have ongoing contact with so many of their potential customers. This is a marketeer or business owner's dream.

IS SOCIAL MEDIA ACTUALLY WORKING FOR BUSINESS?

It is evident that the majority of major brands are running successful social media marketing campaigns. These brands are investing huge amounts of money, time, and resources into this type of marketing. However, you don't have to go too far to see whether social media marketing is actually working for business. Simply ask yourself these questions:

• Would you prefer to buy a product if you knew that a friend or somebody you know had tried it?
• Would you prefer to buy a product from a business or person that you do know rather than a one you don't know?
• If you were thinking of buying a product from a business you had no history with, would you go and look to see if they had a social media site and find out what other people were saying about their product?

If you answered yes to these questions then you can be pretty sure that social media marketing does actually work for businesses. It has to, doesn't it?

WHY SO MANY BUSINESSES ARE GETTING IT WRONG

Even though most business owners have heard how powerful social media marketing can be, the majority are still unsure as to how to use it to benefit their business. So many Social media account have been created with enthusiasm only to be abandoned a couple of months, even weeks, down the line. Others are painstakingly posting consistently every day but posting the wrong type of content without a clue how to get their followers to buy their products. Many businesses are just paying lip service and seem to think that displaying a few social media icons on their site is enough to miraculously increase their revenue, and some are not even connected to any networks at all. Although on the face of it social media marketing seems free, it actually takes a sizeable investment of man hours, and if you are getting it wrong, you may as well be throwing a great deal of money out of the window. Here are some common reasons why so many businesses are getting it wrong:

Not 100% committed and convinced

Many businesses are not convinced that it actually works at all and therefore are not prepared to put in the time it takes to learn how to plan and implement the effective strategies it takes to build a successful campaign. As a result, their campaign falls flat and they simply give up after a few months.

Little or no understanding about how social media marketing works

Many still think that setting up a profile and putting an icon on their website is what it's all about. They may even post a few status updates and post some pictures of their product in the hope that their website is suddenly going to be inundated with new traffic and think that these new visitors are miraculously going to convert into customers.

They don't understand the fact that fans and followers are worthless unless they know what to do with them

Just because a business has maybe 1000 or 30,000 fans or followers, it does not mean this will automatically transfer to their balance sheet. Fans are just fans, and as long a business doesn't know what do with those fans, they will stay as fans and not customers.

Not understanding the psychology behind buying decisions

They have absolutely no idea about the psychology behind how and why people make buying decisions and, therefore, do not know how to use this knowledge to their advantage in their campaign.

Lack of clear goals

Aimlessly sharing content on their network without setting specific and measurable goals is just a waste of time and resources.

Not having a system to capture and convert leads

Building a following is almost useless if those followers are not visiting the business' website or subscribing to the newsletter so that they can be converted into paying customers. Many businesses are still not making lead capture one of their main goals.

Unrealistic expectations

Social media is a long-term strategy. It needs to be an integral part of a business' marketing plan, and today, it's as important as any other daily task a business may undertake. It is not a one-size-fits-all solution and is not a solution for overnight success. It takes careful planning and long-term commitment.

The wrong audience

It's no good having a huge number of followers if they are not interested in buying your product.

Not enough followers

The majority of businesses are going to need a sizeable audience to make any impact at all. Although engagement is important, unless a business has a healthy number of followers, it's not going to be a great deal of benefit.

Not being proactive

Many businesses seem to assume that people are just going to press the 'like' or 'follow' button on their blog or website. Unfortunately it doesn't work like that and people generally need a good reason or incentive to follow a business, unless it's a very well-known brand.

Trying to push their products all the time

This is not what social media marketing is about. Businesses that continually push their products are just missing the whole point of how social media marketing works and will lose followers as a result.

Posting too little, posting too often, or posting the wrong content altogether

If you post too much, your posts will be considered spam. If you post too little, you will just be forgotten. If you post the wrong content, you will not attract the right audience which may harm your brand. The top three reasons for losing followers are:

i.) The company posts too frequently

ii.) The business pushes their products too much

iii.) The business posts offensive content

CHAPTER TWO

How to Run a Successful Instagram Marketing Campaign, an Overview

ONCE YOU HAVE made the decision to be 100% committed to your campaign, you fully understand the theory behind it and you plan and implement the strategies and tactics outlined in this book your business is going to reap the benefits and you will in time develop an extremely valuable asset. One thing is for certain if you choose to ignore social media you can be sure that your competition will not and you'll be allowing them to steal the advantage. Social media is a powerful way to increase your revenue by driving sales, increasing customer loyalty and building your brand while at the same time pushing down your cost of sales, marketing, customer service and much more. Now let's get started!

So how do you leverage the power of social media and put it to work to benefit your business and produce amazing results? This chapter is designed to give you a brief overview about what is required to build a successful campaign so that as and when you read each chapter it will make more sense. Every aspect of this overview and everything you need to do and implement will be mapped out clearly for you in the subsequent chapters.

The opportunity to reach an unlimited number of new contacts and prospects is available to every business today. You can safely say that your prospects are out there and all you need to do is know where to find them, how to connect with them and then how to capture and convert them into your customers.

Successful businesses are using Instagram and the other social media platforms in a totally different way to that of traditional methods of marketing. With Instagram marketing there is no need to employ pushy sales techniques. Once you put the essential work, planning and system in place you will find your products are practically selling themselves and your prospects are buying your products and becoming your brand advocates as a natural progression from your initial contact with them. The whole process is straight forward and as long as you carry out the necessary background work, planning and preparation you can make it work for your business.

Know what you want

You need to have a good idea where you want your business to be in the next 1−3 years, if you don't know what you want then it is unlikely that your business will achieve anywhere near its potential. When you have a clear vision for your business it helps you to focus and create the necessary goals you need to put into place to achieve that vision.

Define your business and your brand and your target audience

Brands establish customer loyalty and Instagram offers you a huge opportunity to build your brand. In order to communicate in the right way you need to create and consistently deliver the right message and brand experience to your prospects and customers. To do this you need to define your business and define and understand your target audience so you can create your brand.

Plan, plan, plan

Social media is not a quick fix, the majority of businesses start a campaign and then fall by the wayside. If you want to grow your business then careful planning is required which involves: creating your mission statement, setting clear and measurable goals and objectives, planning your system for lead capture and planning your content strategy in line with who and what your target audience want. Putting a good plan and system into place will take all the guess work, worry and stress out of your campaign and give you confidence and direction. You will find that the campaign will be almost running itself and working like a machine producing leads and customers. Without a carefully crafted plan your campaign is extremely unlikely to succeed and you will waste huge amounts of time and resources.

Prepare your business

Before launching your campaign you need to prepare your whole business so your brand and your brand message is evident throughout. You will need to communicate your brand through everything your do or say including all your marketing material, brochures, promotional material, your website, your blog and your email.

Your website is one of the best sales people you can have, it works 24/7 and can turn up in your customer's home at the click of a mouse. When your prospect arrives on your website you need to make them feel they have arrived at the right place and that you understand their needs and can either provide a solution or give them exactly what they want. If you already have a website then you need to check it has all the necessary features it takes to grab your visitors attention, deliver the right message, capture them and convert them into customers. Statistics prove that unless a business has a clever method of capturing leads then the majority of visitors to a website will leave without buying anything or ever returning again. Therefore before even starting your Instagram campaign you will need to check or create your website so that it does the job it is supposed to which is to capture leads and convert them into customers.

Set up your email campaign

Email is still one of the most effective methods of converting leads and therefore you will need to set up an account with an email service provider and plan your email campaign so you can continue to build a relationship with your prospect, build trust and sell your products.

Set up your Instagram bio

Your Instagram bio will in many cases be the first impression your prospects have about your business and is as important as your website or blog. The aim of your bio is to introduce yourself to other users and persuade them to follow you by showing them your best images which promote your brand and appeal to their interests. You then need to continue to communicate and build a relationship with them through their feed and hopefully through their email. Your followers may not return to your bio after their initial visit so you need to make sure your communicate your message effectively and grab your audience's interest and attention.

Create your Instagram posting calendar

Social media is not like traditional forms of advertising so frequently pushing your products, posting adverts and plugging your business is not going to work and is likely to lose you followers. One of the most important things you are going to have to do for a successful Instagram campaign is to regularly produce and post compelling images that your audience actually wants to engage with by liking and commenting. Instagram marketing is all about selling without selling and the aim of producing content is not to directly sell your products but to do the following:

- Boost traffic to your blog or website, generate, capture and nurture leads.
- Create brand awareness.
- Constantly remind your audience of your brand so when they are ready to buy they buy from you.
- Improve your ranking in the search engines.
- Create engagement, build relationships and encourage your audience to share your content with their friends.
- Support others by liking and commenting. Even though Instagram does no offer the functionality to share other posts on Instagram you can install apps that will repost other peoples

images and give credit to the original poster.

- Stand out as a thought leader and build your reputation as an expert in your industry.
- Create such a great experience that your audience stays liking your profile and continuing to see your images which builds and encourage brand loyalty.

Your content is where you can connect with your audience through their interests and passions. Your quality of content needs to be outstanding and you need to delight your audience with the best possible fresh, new and compelling material, excellence is what you should be aiming for every time you post. The biggest thing to remember is that you need to tailor all your content to your audience's desires and needs.

Once you are absolutely clear about who your target audience is, what makes them tick, and what their values and aspirations are you can determine what subjects and topics they will be interested in. The majority of the content you post will need to be about their needs and not yours. There is nothing more off putting and likely to lose you followers than continually posting about your business and shouting about your products or services. Of course if you are in the business of selling beautiful things you can do this but you also have to do this in a way that is interesting and not in a pushy way you that becomes bad noise to your customer. Remember your followers are mostly on Instagram to be delighted and entertained with beautiful images and to be social. If your posts ruin their social experience they will associate your brand with a bad experience and it won't be long before you start losing your followers and potential customers.

When you have decided on the subjects and topics you are going to create images about, then you will need to create a Instagram posting calendar which will help you to consistently deliver this high quality images. You will need to incorporate everything in this calendar including any events you are planning, any special industry events, public holidays, blog posts, videos and offers or contests you may be planning. You then need to map it all out so you know exactly how you are going to promote them on Instagram with the functionality you have available.

Build a sizeable and highly targeted following

The main aim of building your audience is to grow a community of followers who are interested in your products, will engage with your content and become advocates for your brand. In order to have any impact at all you are going to need a sizeable number of targeted followers on Instagram. Building your audience is going to be an ongoing task and involve many different strategies all covered in this book. The size and time it takes to build your audience will depend on the time and resources you have available. However, do not get overwhelmed and compare yourself with those who have got thousands of followers, it's more important to concentrate your efforts on targeting the right audience and then delighting them with great content. This way you will benefit from everything that goes with a highly engaged audience by delivering a great brand experience and you will find your audience naturally growing in a very positive way.

9. The essential day to day activity

To build a strong presence, build trust, build relationships and reputation you will need to be active and nurture your followers. Social media is not a one way street, it's an ongoing two way communication, it's about going out and showing that you are interested in what others have to say and it's about building community and getting your brand out there in the most positive light possible. Here are some of the things you will need to do on a day to day basis:

- Consistently post high quality images.
- Follow your followers.
- Engage, comment and reply.
- Show your audience you value and respect them.
- Follow influencers in your niche.
- Deal with negative comments.

Analysing and measuring your campaign results

This book is all about how to make Instagram work for your business and the only way you are going to find out if it is working or not is by constantly monitoring and analysing your results. You will need to constantly check your results against the goals and objectives you have set. Once you know what is working and what is not then you can adjust and steer your campaign accordingly, to achieve more positive results.

CHAPTER THREE

GETTING STARTED ON INSTAGRAM

"INSTAGRAM IS A fast, beautiful and fun way to share your life with friends and family." This is Instagram's official description but is now a whole lot more and with 150 million users and still growing, Instagram has become a powerhouse for marketing any brand and has the ability to connect on an emotional and personal level.

The Instagram mobile app was launched in 2010 solely as a photo sharing site and managed to gain 400 million users to date. In June 2013 it incorporated video sharing, allowing its users to create and share video lasting up to 15 seconds. In September 2012 Facebook acquired Instagram with its 13 employees for $1 billion in cash and stocks, it was the largest acquisition deal to date!

Instagram's unique feature is that it confines images to a square shape and allows its users to add digital filters to enhance their photos and then share them with their friends or followers. Users can also share their images on other social networks like Twitter, Facebook, Tumblr and Flickr.

In order to appreciate how Instagram can work for businesses it is essential to understand why Instagram is so successful. The answer is that Instagram has combined the power of the image with the power of social media and the launch of iphone and android devices with their high quality camera and video capability. Users can now easily take pictures of what they love and see, and then share them with their friends and followers and other social networks instantly. Everything about the app is simple, immediate and fun and users can take quite ordinary pictures and quickly make them into something quite remarkable with the filters and effects. The single feed lets users focus on just one single image which they can like and comment on easily.

Instagram has opened up a whole new world of intrigue, discovery and interaction and people get to see things that they would not ordinarily see and connect with people they wouldn't usually connect with. It is no wonder it is now one of the most popular mobile apps in the world.

As one of the fastest growing social networks Instagram is definitely a platform that marketeers and business owners need to pay attention to. Like Pinterest, Instagram has let businesses build their brands through the power of the image and has given businesses the ability to build their brand by connecting with their followers in an emotional and personal way. Some businesses have literally been able to catapult their business from little to well know in no time all. With a constant stream of photos that personalize and represent their business' personality they are now able to connect with their prospective customers in a whole new way by delivering a new visual experience and creating memorable brands. Brands like Top Shop, Gucci ,Virgin, Burberry, Audi, Starbucks, Red Bull and Levi's all realized the power of the Instagram early on and continue to grow their audience and keep them interested with regular uploads.

Images are hugely important to brands for marketing as most people are visually wired and images tend to appeal to the emotions. Beautiful and interesting shots can quickly attract followers, show off a product and help users identify and relate with a brand much more easily than with text. Images are also far more likely to be remembered and by reaching their audience with images in a fun light hearted way, brands can encourage interaction. With behind the scenes images businesses can offer their followers a degree of transparency and authenticity which helps them to build trust. When people feel personally connected with a brand or business they are more likely to purchase from that brand when they are ready to buy.

Instagram's audience is quite young compared with that of Facebook and Twitter and the majority of users are between 18 and 35 so it is the perfect platform for any small business who wants to promote their product or service to this younger audience on a smaller budget. Another really amazing statistic is that over half of its users use Instagram daily. Instagram users just love the platform and it is all very much about soul, emotion and personality. It's not until you start using the platform yourself that you can truly appreciate and experience the thriving and positive communities that are present on Instagram and realize the possibilities for promoting any business.

Like all the social media platforms Instagram takes time, dedication and commitment. Although it is simple to use you still need to find ideas and create a good deal of content to succeed on this platform. Posting photos has to be frequent but not as frequent as other platforms. Once a day is probably optimal but some brands are even successful posting less often.

THE BENEFITS OF INSTAGRAM FOR BUSINESS.

Before you go ahead and set up your account you need decide exactly what you want to gain for your business from Instagram and you need to have a clear idea of what your goals and objectives are. Here is a list of possible benefits and uses of Instagram for business:

To find new customers increase
If you have products which are aimed at the 18 −35 age group then you are most probably going to find them on Instagram. The percentage of male to female users is fairly evenly split. There are exceptions to this in the Far East where the audience is female dominated and in Saudi Arabia where it tends to be male dominated.

To stay in contact with your customers

What better way to stay in contact with your customers and keep them coming back to buy your products than by posting images. It's less intrusive and probably more interesting than email and keeps your product or service fresh in their mind. Also a great way to communicate new products and new offers .

Drive traffic to your website or blog

If you find the right audience for your products and you are posting beautiful images of those products then it is natural that your followers are going to want to check out where they can buy those products. Instagram is the perfect place to showcase your products and get traffic to your website.

To increase overall awareness of your brand

If you know who your audience are and you know their needs and desires you can connect with your audience emotionally by giving them the content they want and then connecting with them emotionally. Once you have been successful doing this you can really succeed in building your brand. Posting photos on a regular basis is a sure way to widen your reach and introduce your brand to new potential customers in a visual way. Once you have new followers you can build their trust by keeping in contact visually and they will be more likely to remember you when they next go to make a purchase.

Market Research

Similar to Pinterest, Instagram can given you huge insight into your target audience and what they like. If you find and follow your audience on Instagram you can discover so much information about them with the images that they post. The more information you find out about our audience the more likely you will be able to give them what they want. When you connect with them emotionally through the type of images that they can identify with then you will be onto a winning formula.

To promote a new product or event

If you have built up a loyal following and you have a new product, book or event to launch what better way to introduce it than with a simple image or sequence of images. Posting images will constantly remind your followers to go take a peep at your website or go along to your event.

Build a stronger social presence on other platforms

Instagram is an excellent place to find more of your audience and can be a great way to build your following on other social networks like Facebook or Twitter.

Build subscribers on your opt-in list

Email is still one of the most powerful tools in converting leads to customers. Instagram can be a very effective way to get followers to join your opt-in as long as you have the right system in place. To do this you need to drive your followers to an external page and offer them an incentive to join your opt-in.

To create viral photos & videos

There is no better way to increase awareness of your brand than by creating viral content. Photos or videos of cute kittens, animals, babies and animals doing funny things are incredibly viral. If you are good at finding and creating images like this, then it could be a very effective way of getting your brand noticed.

To integrate with other social platforms

You may find that Instagram works well with other platforms. You could for instance use Facebook or Twitter to promote a contest on Instagram.

To connect with your audience personally

The Instagram 15 second video functionality is a great way to connect with your followers and make a personal connection without having to worry about high video production costs. You can say and demonstrate a great deal in these bite size videos. Also because your followers know they are only short videos they may be more likely to watch.

SETTING UP YOUR PROFILE

Setting up your Instagram is free, quick and easy. Simply download the app from the app store if you have an iphone, or Google play if you are on Android. You will need to set up your account with a user name and password and then fill out the profile information and upload your profile image with either your logo or a photo of yourself.

Your username is like your signature and needs to clearly represent your brand and be similar to your usernames on other social networks. Try and make your username as short and easy as possible for users to type in and if possible make sure your name is the same as your username.

When it comes to adding your website address you need to remember that your profile is the only place that allows for clickable links and the only place for your website URL. Instagram does not allow for clickable links in posts, comments and captions. You need to take this into consideration when deciding which web page you are going to be sending your followers to.

Having the right bio can really help to increase the number of followers you have and you have 150 characters to tempt them to do this. When creating your bio you need to think about what your audience wants and the sorts of things that they are interested in and then mention these. Try and include keywords from your niche and make it as interesting and punchy as possible. You can also use emoji characters if you want to brighten up your bio, this can work especially well if they tie in with your branding. Having a look at some popular brands and personalities on Instagram can really help to inspire you, you can do this by searching on Instagram or on Google.

You can then connect your account with Facebook, Twitter, Flickr, Tumblr and Foursquare by going to the gear icon on the top right and then 'Share Settings' under preferences which helps you to share your photos to other services and also allows your friends on Facebook to find you. It will also create a news story for anyone who follows you on Facebook and has their Facebook and Instagram account connected. You will then be offered the option to find your Facebook friends and invite any contacts from your phone and then you will be given the opportunity to follow some people on Instagram. Make sure you set your account to public. Your profile is also available now on the web and will show a selection of your recently uploaded photos above your profile photo and bio. To have a look at what some of the big brands have done simply type in www.instagram/username

Starter Images

Even though your Bio is important the images you upload are even more important and this is what is really going to be the deciding factor between whether users follow you or not. The best thing you can do for your business on Instagram is show people why they should get to know you. Before you start building your audience you will need to have uploaded at least 21 images to create some interest and attract users to follow you. The next chapter is dedicated to tips about how and what to post on Instagram.

INSTAGRAM BASICS

Now you have set up your profile you need to familiarise yourself with the app. Here is a quick guide to finding your way around Instagram:

The Instagram menu

The Instagram menu is situated along the bottom and is made up of the profile tab, the camera tab, the explore tab, the home tab and news.

- **The profile tab** The profile tab is the last icon on the bottom menu and is where you can edit your profile and also shows the images you have uploaded, you can either view these in a grid by clicking the grid icon above the images or in a vertical feed by clicking the icon with 3 horizontal lines. Above the images you can also navigate to the 'photo map' which lets others explore where you have taken your photos. This is an option and the 'adding your location' function is turned off by default.

- **The Camera tab** The camera tab is where you can take photos with the Instagram app or share photos from your library.

- **The Explore tab** The Explore tab is where you can find new and interesting people to follow. You can either search by username or by hashtag. You can also view a gallery of images that have been selected by Instagram who have based their selection on the things that the people you follow have liked as well as content that is trending on Instagram.

- **The Home tab** The Home tab shows your feed of images posted by you and your followers. This is where you can like, comment and mention others in the text area under the images.

Like To like an image simply click the heart icon under the image, or double tap the image and your user name will be added to the likers under the image.

Comment To comment simply add your comment to the text space under the image. You can also add emoji icons to comments which can really draw attention to your comments.

To delete a comment you have made on a post simply tap on the comment under the image and then swipe from right to left on your comment and choose to delete.

@Mention The @mention can be used in the comments section on Instagram for replying to comments and thanking. Thanking your followers for commenting is a common and good practice on Instagram, simply add the @ sign before the username. You can also use the @mention to tag or mention users in the caption area of your photo.

Instagram Direct Instagram allows you send images up to 15 users privately which will not appear in the News feed. You can access Instagram Direct by tapping the icon on top right of your home feed.

TAKING PHOTOS ON INSTAGRAM

When using Instagram you can take photos using the Instagram app or select an image from your image library from your iphone or android device.

- To take a picture simply tap the screen to focus and then tap the big blue button.

- To zoom in and crop your image simply move and pinch the photo to whichever scale you want within the frame and then press 'crop' on the top right.

- Click 'next' on the top right and you can then jazz up your photo with any of the 20 filters available.

- When you add a filter you can also add a border (Amaro, Rise and Valencia filters do not have borders.) Simply tap the square above the image to add the border and tap again to take away the border.

- You can also add blur, tear drop and tilt effects to your image and if you want to make your image more vibrant and to bring out details simply tap the sun icon on the right.

- You can add more interest to your image if you like by rotating it, simply tap on the tilted square image on the left.

- Click next and then add your caption and hashtags. You can tag people in the photo if you like by using the @ symbol followed by the username and you can add your photo to the photo map if you wish. If you want to draw someones attention to the image you can @mention them in the caption. In the caption you can add a URL but it will not be clickable.

- You can then select which other networks you want to share with, Facebook, Twitter, Tumblr and/or Flickr. To share with Foursquare you need to add your photo to the map.

- Finally when you are ready click 'Share' and your image will be published to the feed and all the networks you chose to share it with.

CREATING VIDEOS FOR INSTAGRAM

Instagram gives you another way to share your moments with video. You can either create videos using the Instagram video function or upload videos from your phone and then like photos you can add filters which have been created especially for video. The 15 second videos are a great way to show your followers how to do things and also a great way of bringing your brand to life. This is yet another opportunity for brands to reach their audiences and build a connection at minimal cost.

CHAPTER FOUR

CREATING THE BEST VISUAL EXPERIENCE FOR YOUR FOLLOWERS

IN ORDER TO build a thriving community of brand advocates and customers who want to interact with your content, sign up to your newsletter and buy your products you are going to need to build trust, loyalty and likeability. The only way to do this is by communicating with them on regular basis in the right way and by consistently delivering the highest possible quality content which will grab their attention, appeal to their interests and add real value to their lives. Once your followers start engaging with your content, you will start building trust and start converting them into customers.

So that you can build a real connection with your followers you will need to think of ideas for images or videos which will appeal to your audience emotionally and get them to make friends with your brand. Your goal here needs to be to inspire and interest your followers, let them have fun and above all make them smile. Your audience want to see the personality of your business and your human side. Even businesses that are considered to be quite dull have been successful in driving interaction with humorous images or videos.

As with any social media you need to have a deep understanding of your audience. Hopefully by the time you have created your profile you will already have a clear idea of who your ideal customer is and what subjects and topics they are interested in. This whole topic about your target audience will be covered in more detail in the chapter about planning, later one.

With the help of sites like Instagram and Pinterest you can find out exactly what makes your audience tick. Never has there been so much opportunity to research what your customers are interested in than with a site like Instagram. You can gain huge insight into what your target audience's interests are and what they like by simply looking at their profiles and seeing what sort of images they are posting and what they are liking and commenting on. Instagram lets you dig even deeper into peoples personalities as users tend to share much more, they share their lives, creativity and feelings, probably more than on any other social network. By visiting the profiles of your target audience you will be able to see what types of images they are uploading, liking and sharing. This information is like gold and will not only help you with marketing and your building brand on Instagram but also on other social media platforms as well.

In this chapter you are going to learn about the different types of post, different types of content and tips on how help you create the best experience for your connections and followers so you can receive the highest engagement. Before you start posting here is a list of questions you should ask yourself about your audience when planning your content:

Who are the audiences you need to connect with?
Are these audiences using Instagram?
Are they following your competition on Instagram?
What are they interested in? What are they posting?
What are they looking for ?
What sort of topics would appeal to them?
What are the problems they have that they need solving?

Your competition on Instagram
You can find out a great deal of information about your target audience

from your competition as well. See what images they are uploading and see what their followers are liking and posting. It maybe they are not doing a great job and you maybe you will see ways you can do it better. It's definitely worthwhile spending as much time as possible researching your competitors.

IDEAS FOR DIFFERENT IMAGES & VIDEOS

You may be wondering how you are going to consistently produce and deliver a stream of compelling images to your audience on a regular basis for the foreseeable future. However once you have picked your topic of interest you will surprised how one idea will lead to another and you will be able to produce numerous images. When you post your images your followers will see these updates on their homepage feed and they can like and comment on your images.

Unless you are an artist or a fashion brand it is unlikely that your followers are going to want to see a constant stream of product pictures, this would be incredibly boring and will not help you to promote your brand or get the following you need for success on this platform. In order to build a real connection with your followers you will need to think of ideas for images or videos which will appeal to your audience emotionally and get them to make friends with your brand. Your goal here needs to be to inspire and interest your followers, let them have fun and above all make them smile. Your audience want to see the personality of your business and your human side. Even businesses that are considered to be quite dull have been successful in driving interaction with humorous images or videos. With Instagram your uploads need to offer a variety of images to spark interaction and keep your followers interested and engaged. It really is advisable to follow some top brands who are doing it right on Instagram simply go to http://50.nitrogr.am/ and you can see the top 50 brands. Here are some ideas for the types of images you can upload:

Relatable images

Relatable images are one of the most popular types of images and drive likes and comments. Relatable content is anything that your target audience can relate to and identify with, it's when your audience sees a piece of content and immediately think, "Yes, I know exactly what they mean and that is exactly how I feel when this happens." It's incredibly powerful because this content is immediately communicating to your audience that you understand them and you feel their pain or joy and you can empathise with them. With relatable content you are communicating with them on quite a deep level which all helps to build relationships and trust. This is why Someecards is so successful, most of their content is relatable.

Emotive images

Evoking an emotional response is an essential ingredient for success on Instagram. If you create content that evokes a strong positive emotional response it will help your audience associate that emotion with your brand. Content like this is very memorable and if you can make people feel something by posting an image, text or a video this can really help in building your brand and creating powerful associations. Evoking any of the primary emotions be it surprise, joy, or fear, sadness, anger or disgust is a certain way to get people sharing your content. Pictures that tug your heartstrings are great and images of cute animals and children are a real winner on Instagram, people also love pictures of food and beautiful places.

Educational images

Posting images about your subject is invaluable, this will help you to stand out as a thought leader and expert in your field. If your content is valuable and useful then your followers are likely to keep coming back for more and are likely to share your content too.

Informative images

This could be about letting your followers know about something that is happening, like a Webinar, a book launch, trade show or event in the area, or a special offer, or any information that will be of use or value to them.

Entertaining/amusing images

Social media is all about being social and having fun and people love seeing funny stuff. Posting funny images that appeal to the sense of humor of your target audience will always be a winner and will drive likes and comments.

Seasonal Images

Posting images relating to important holidays and annual celebrations is a really good way to stay connected with your audience. If you have an international audience then being aware of their holidays and religious celebrations will go a long way in building relationships.

Inspiring and motivational content

The truth is everyone has a bad day sometimes and needs a little bit of motivation or cheering up. A motivational quote will help to lift your audience and can really help to connect with them. If you know what your audience wants, what they aspire to and what their frustrations are then it is likely that you will be able to motivate them by posting content which inspires them. These types of post are also very shareable especially if put together with a colorful and inspiring image like a cartoon or photo.

Employee and behind the scenes content

People love to see what is going on behind the scenes. Giving your audience a behind the scenes view of your business helps to keeps your business and brand looking real, authentic and adds human interest. If you have news about your employees and the great things they are doing then post it. Maybe they have been involved in a fundraiser or they have won an employee of the month award. You can show pictures of your office, your employees, the sandwich girl bringing your lunch or the CEO shaking their booty at the company bash. You can get really creative here and this is where you can really tell the story behind your brand. Daily events happening in your business may seem mundane to you but to your audience they may be incredibly interesting. For example, if you are a restaurant you could show the delivery of one of your ingredients or maybe show one of your signature dishes and give the ingredients or produce an Instagram video showing how it is made.

Statistics

People love statistics which relate to their niche. If your business is B2B then posting statistics can gain a great deal of interest especially if they are displayed in a visually appealing way like with an infographic or graph. They are often shared if they are translated into a useful tip for your followers.

Special offers

Social media is a great way to get the message out about the special offers you have running but you will need to be careful not to post them too often or they just appear like advertising and bad noise in your audience's news feed. You need to make sure that what you are offering is of real value, that it is exclusive to your followers and you are offering them a deadline to redeem the offer.

Contests and sweepstakes

Contests and sweepstakes are always a great way to gain popularity, grow your audience, build your brand and build your opt-in email list. With contests your audience can have great fun with your brand and they can also create high levels of engagement. Creating and running contests will be covered in more detail later on.

Caption this

Posting a photo and then asking your audience to caption it is a really effective and light hearted way to drive engagement and you could also turn this into a contest. You can use your own images or images from stock photo sites or sites like Flickr, make sure you check the terms of uses and choose images which are either interesting, humorous or inspiring.

Internet Memes

Meme comes from the greek word 'mimema' which means something imitated. An internet meme is a style, action or idea which spreads virally across the internet. They can take the form of images, videos or hashtags. There are plenty of tools and apps out there to help you create memes such as www.memegen.com and imgur.com which are popular ones.

Your blog

Posting an image which relates to your latest blog post can be a very effective way of getting your followers onto your website or Blog. Make sure you always include an image to provoke interest and asking a question can create intrigue and curiosity.

Greetings

Simply posting an attractive image or a wishing your followers good morning, good night or enjoy your weekend will go a long way in breaking the ice and building relationships. These types of posts help to make positive associations with your brand.

Product photos

Unless you are really artistic or a fashion brand or have a creative collection of some sort then it is a good idea to follow the 80/20 rule, 20% product photos and 80% other photos relating and telling the story of your brand.

You really need to get creative with product photos and try and make them as interesting as possible. Taking pictures of your staff or your customers wearing or using your products can add interest and a personal touch rather than perhaps the product on its own. You could ask your followers to upload pictures of themselves using or wearing your product and have a follower of the day. This can be incredibly powerful and creates real buzz around your products and brand.

Event Photos

Photos before, during and after an event can create real hype around an event, exhibition or trade show. These type of photos make your followers feel part of the event and can help to draw them into a more personal connection with your business.

Charity events

If your business involves itself with charity then show your followers with your images as this is a great way to show the more human side of your business.

Customer focused photos

Photos of your customers using, wearing or eating your products is a great way to connect with your audience in a fun way. Some brands have really mastered this and have created high levels of interest and engagement and seen their follower numbers soar as a result. You can get your customers to post their photos with a certain hashtag so you can find them and also make this part of a contest.

Photos of your city/art/anything

People just love looking at interesting images and you may see lots of interesting and beautiful things in your day to day life. The sort of images you post will depend on your audience type and the image that you brand wants to promote but most people like beautiful things. It might be a beautiful sunset, flower or piece of art or architecture. If you think it's a great shot, chances are other people will too. Use Instagram as a window for people to look through and see you and your brand.

How to photos and videos

Instagram is a great way to visually show people how to do things, either by uploading a sequence of images or one image which has been split into 4. Restaurants can showcase their best dishes and then list the ingredients or create short videos. The possibilities are endless and can be incredibly inspiring for people.

Send sneak previews
Sending your new products to a group of people can make them feel they are in an elite group. People love to think they have the insider information or are the first to know about something.

Select a specific color or colors for you images
Some brands have been incredibly successful in creating galleries on Instagram that keep to one or a few specific colors. This can really help with branding and is very memorable for followers.

Introductory videos
Using short 15 second video feature on Instagram to post your own introduction video is a great way to reach your audience in the most personal way.

Teaser videos
It may be that you have some great content on YouTube and therefore you could create a teaser video on Instagram to promote your Channel.

TOP TIPS FOR POSTING ON INSTAGRAM
To make your Instagram marketing super successful here are a few tips on posting on Instagram:

Follow brands and your competition
If you start by following brands then you can see how they are using Instagram. You may be able to adopt different techniques and ideas. Also keep an eye on what your competition are doing. You can be pretty sure they will be doing the same. Using Nitrogram to find and follow brands can be really helpful, Nitrogram is an analytics and engagement platform that lists the top 50 brands on Instagram.

Create a location page

This is particularly useful if you have a bricks and mortar business. Just before uploading your photo you have the opportunity to tag that photo in the geotag field. That photo will then appear on a location page in Instagram and will help your business to get found by other instagrammers in your area, they will be able to view your images and hopefully as a result will either visit your business or start following you. Currently location search results are provided by Foursquare's location database so you will need to sign up for Foursquare in the app store or on Google Play. When you have done that go to the check-in tab and search for the place you want to add and then tap 'Add this place.' You should then be able to search for it on the location screen in Instagram. You can then add your photo, tap the place name above the photo and you can see the location you have created. This is where all your photos tagged with this location will appear.

Hashtags

Hashtags are big big big on Instagram. Hashtags help like minded people connect on Instagram and help people categorise and organize their photos. The purpose of hashtags is to help get your image found by connecting your photo with photos that other Instagram users have posted. When you put the hashtag sign before a word or phrase it becomes clickable and brings up all the content relating to that hashtag.

There are two ways of using hashtags on Instagram. Firstly for discoverability and secondly to find other follower made content and to extend your reach by appearing in search when people are searching for relevant topics. With hashtags you need to be as specific, relevant and descriptive as possible. To find out what is trending on Instagram check sites like Webstagram and then you can create content around popular hashtags.

Unlike other social sites, multiple hashtags do work on Instagram so you are safe to post more than just a few and many are successful posting up to ten to twelve.

When you have a sizeable audience you can create a hashtag specifically for your brand as well. Simply create a really amusing and unique hashtag and you may find people join in and then every time that hashtag is used it is associated with your brand.

Top Tip

If you use the same hashtags frequently then to save you having to type them out again and again it's a good idea to copy them onto a notes application on your mobile device so that they can be pasted into the caption area when you are posting.

Descriptions, URLS and product codes

Make sure to add descriptions to the caption area and if your are featuring products from a web page then include the URL to that specific product or a product code.

Add 'calls to action' to descriptions

One of the main advantages of social media is it gives consumers a voice and the opportunity to give you feedback about products which makes encouraging your followers to comment of paramount importance. Posting questions is a great way to encourage comments and engagement and makes your followers feel valued.

Add 'calls to action' to image

One of the main advantages of social media is it gives consumers a voice and the opportunity to give you feedback about products, so encouraging your followers to comment is of paramount importance. Posting questions is a great way to encourage comments and get your followers talking about your business. Asking questions also makes your followers feel their opinions are valued.

Adding a call to action to an image is a great way to get followers to interact and is a much more effective than adding them to your description. Obviously you cannot do this on every image but occasionally this can work very well.

Post regularly and consistently

Success is unlikely to come overnight with Instagram. It will take time to build your following, so you need to stay with it and post consistently but not madly, once a day is optimal and more if you have the content.

According to statistics videos gain seven times more engagement than photos. You can upload video for up to 15 seconds and it's a great way of building that emotional connection with your followers and stamping your personality on your brand.

Promos and discount Codes

A very effective way to get your followers over to your site is to offer promo codes and discounts. Don't forget to hashtag your special promotion images with #promocode. To find out what other businesses are doing simply search #promocode and have a look at some of the images.

Encourage followers to mention their friends

There is no share function on Instagram so getting your content to get seen by non followers is harder. However some brands have been successful in getting their followers to mention their friends in the comments with an @mention. You could do this by simply asking them to tell their friends about a certain promotion or competition or by asking if they know a friend who likes a certain thing.

Don't hog the feed

Constantly posting images is a sure way to get you unfollowed, as users want to see a variety of images from different users. Instagram is all about discovery, wonderment and inspiration so people do not want to keep seeing more of the same.

Add logos to images
Adding logos to images can help with branding, however you need to make sure you keep it as small as possible so not to take over the image and ruin the experience.

TIPS FOR TAKING YOUR PHOTOS
The most important thing on Instagram is posting beautiful images. The reason people love this app is because photos allow us to see the world in a different way. So if you have a beautiful product what better way to showcase it than with a beautiful picture on Instagram. I can not emphasize enough the importance of high quality shots, you have about 1 second to get your audiences attention with an image so it has to be good. You really don't have to be an expert photographer or graphic designer to create amazing images on Instagram, There are numerous applications for both Android and iPhone that can help you enhance your images. However before you even go to any of these apps there a very simple things you can do to make your photos pop and capture the word in a way that people have not seen it before:

1. Keep it simple. The best images are often the most simple. If you over complicate, things can start looking messy, cluttered and unattractive.

2. When taking pictures of products, make sure you have excellent natural light and that light is behind you and shining on the object. This way you avoid getting shadows and also the light will make the colors look more vibrant and beautiful. This piece of advice is for product photos but actually other general interest shots can look great with shadows.

3. Take close up images and zoom in on one object rather than taking a distant shot of a few items.

4. Try unique angles, this can make a huge difference to your images and can give your image a completely different perspective. A great effect can be created by pointing your camera upwards at the subject. Once pointing your camera up you can move it around to create even more different angles. Doing this can help you capture the world and show it is a way that people have never seen it before.

5. Beautiful Landscape shots can sometimes look more interesting with a subject or object. This can add a story to a photo and adds scale to the image too.

6. Silhouette photos always do well on social media and are great for creating interest, mood and can help to create a story. This is where your subjects are under exposed, you can do this by taking photos with the light in front of you. This is not a good idea for product photos where you want to show them off to their full beauty but is great for adding interest to photos of other objects. For example taking a photo of someone in front of a sunset can create stunning results. The best time for silhouette photography is the morning and the evening.

7. As with silhouettes, shadows can create mood and interest. The camera picks up shadows far more effectively than the human eye and therefore accentuates shadows in the image. Shadows are much larger when the sun is low in the sky so as with silhouettes the best time to take these photos is in the morning or evening.

8. Use reflections to enhance your photos. Reflections can make photos look amazing. Water is great for reflections but any reflective surface can work, for example, ice and shiny surfaces. You may not think you see a great deal of reflections but once you start looking for them you be surprised just how many you start noticing. To take good images you need to get close to the reflective surface and get your phone as low as possible.

8. Definitely always take a few shots and choose the best one.

9. Have fun. Once you start looking for images, you yourself will start seeing the World in a different and more beautiful way.

If you do want to enhance your photos with apps then there are numerous apps available. Adobe Photoshop Express lets you add effects, add borders and alter exposure, saturation, tint, contrast and brightness. Other apps includeApple iPhoto, Aviary, Befunky, Morebeaute, Camera +, Camera awesome, Picfx and Lenslight to name but a few! 'Over' is a great app that lets you layer text over your images and use different fonts and sizes all from your mobile. Diptic, Photoshake and PicFrame let you combine multiple images into a single image, great for how to images, tutorial images and collages. Colour Effects and ColourBlast let you grey out everything in an image except for a selected area that you choose to keep one vivid colour.

If you are creating images with photo shop of any other photo editor then the image size requirement is 612 X 612 pixels.

INSTAGRAM DIRECT FOR BUSINESS

Instagram Direct for business Instagram now lets you send and share private images or videos with individuals and smaller groups of up to 15 people which will not appear in the feed. You can send a direct message to anyone even if they do not follow you. If you send it to someone who does not follow you your message will go in their requests queue and they can either accept your request or not. To do this simply take your photo as usual or select from your camera, add your favorite filter and then tap next and tap on 'direct' at the top of your screen. You then select the individual followers you want to send it to and then press 'send.' This definitely has advantages for businesses and can be used in the following ways for marketing:

Contests You can ask followers to send you their images via direct message rather than adding a hashtag for contest if you wish. This can make the contest easier to administer but may not get you the visibility you are looking for.

Sales Vouchers and Coupons You can use Instagram direct for rewarding your most loyal followers. Send a photo to a select few and thank them for being a great follower with details about a sales voucher or money off coupon.

Incentives interactions Post an image and ask a question and then state that the first 15 to comment will receive details by direct message about either a money off coupon or the details to enter a competition.

Send product photos Send photos of your product or a limited edition with a link where to buy, by direct message.

Ask permission to use your followers images You could use this feature to ask your followers to send you an image of them using your product which you can upload. This can be a win win for you and your followers. You get publicity as they will most probably upload the photo to their feed. This will be very appealing to your followers, suddenly they are promoted to all your followers using your product and they are more than likely to publicize the image that they are in to their friends.

Send sneak previews People love to think they have the insider information or are the first to know about something that is being launched. Sending your new products to a group of people can make them feel they are part of an elite group.

SCHEDULING POSTS ON INSTAGRAM

I love Instagram, it's one of the most fun and inspiring of all the social media sites. However up until recently the only thing I did not love was the inability to schedule my posts. Instagram, for the majority, is a place to post your photos as and when the opportunity to take a beautiful, fun or interesting photo arises. For most users, spontaneity and inspiration is what it's all about, however for businesses it's not so easy to post regularly if you can't schedule in advance. I find that the best time to post is often early evening, but the problem with this is I am often not working at this time so it's a bit of a drag to have to tear myself away from whatever I am doing to create and post to Instagram at this time. I would rather be able to create content in my working hours and and then schedule at the optimum time or whenever I prefer.

I am happy to say that now there are now at least three Apps that offer a way around this problem. Although Instagram still doesn't allow you to actually schedule posts these Apps have found a way by letting you create your posts in advance and then scheduling your posts without violating Instagram's terms of use. You do this by uploading your image to the App and then the App notifies you when to post on Instagram. So basically Instagram still requires the human action of posting but it only takes a tap on your mobile to post to Instagram.

Here's how it works:

1. Find and add the App to your mobile device. The three available are; Hootsuite, Latergramme or Viraltag
2. Choose or create the image you would like in the way you usually do.
3. Upload your image to the app and add your caption and hashtags.
4. Select the time you want to post your image to Instagram.
5. At the scheduled time you receive a push notification on your phone advising you that your image is due to be posted on Instagram
6. Tap on the Push notification on your phone to be directed to the App and then review your post in Instagram
7. Once in Instagram you can add your favorite filters, tag users and add a location as usual. The caption you composed in the App for the image will be copied to your phone's clipboard. Simply tap again and select paste to add the caption.
8. Finally tap and share your image to Instagram as you would usually

do.

For business using these apps is a great bonus. It means you can plan and create your posts in advance which makes it so much easier to post regularly and offer your followers a more consistent brand experience. You now keep your brand in your followers minds with ease.

So here are the Apps in a bit more detail;
Hootsuite

I am a big, big fan of Hootsuite. In addition to the obvious multi platform scheduling benefits it also allows you to monitor all your social media platforms including Instagram. The even better news is it's still free for up to 3 social media accounts. From Hootsuite you can view your own Instagram stream, comment and like as well as view photos of the people you follow. Setting up your streams is really easy on Hootsuite and you can also follow and unfollow accounts from Hootsuite. This takes away the hassle of having to use your mobile as well as your desktop or laptop. Here is a great resource from Hootsuite on how to set all this up

https://hootsuite.com/en-gb/resources/hoot-tip/how-to-add-instagram-to-your-hootsuite-dashboard

Latergramme.me

Later gramme was ahead of the game as first to offer Instagram posting functionality. It's free for one account and allows you to do all of the following:

- Upload posts from your computer, iPhone, Tablet or Android
- Manage Multiple Instagram accounts
- Add team members to collaborate on Instagram accounts
- Search and repost content from the web
- Upload video posts to be scheduled later (this is a paid option)

Viraltag

ViralTag is a tool you can use for sharing and scheduling you images to your social media accounts, Pinterest, Facebook, Linkedin , Twitter and now Instagram. You can also share from your mobile too. Like Buffer you can queue your images to post or schedule them. With Instagram, VitalTag also uses the method above to help you post your content. Plans start from $29 per month.

CHAPTER FIVE

BUILDING YOUR AUDIENCE ON INSTAGRAM

BEFORE YOU START building your audience you will need to have uploaded some images to give your account some starter content and show off your brand's personality. Unless you are a very well known brand then users will be put off by an endless sequence of product images so you need to think very carefully about the story you want to tell and the images you are going to upload to tell that story. Once you are ready and have uploaded a good collection of images to show off your brand you can start building your audience.

Find your friends Instagram offers you the opportunity when you set up your account to invite your Facebook friends and contacts from your phone. Make sure you announce on the other platforms that you are on Instagram, this is crucial to getting you a head start.

Display Instagram badges You can find the code for Instagram badges here http://instagram.com/accounts/badges/ which can easily be embedded in your website or blog.

Display your Instagram handle Make sure you display your handle on your email signature and on all your marketing material.

Announce your profile on other social networks If you are active on other social networks then announce your presence on Instagram and invite your followers over to join you. It is likely that you will grow your reach through their followers and also you can often offer them a different and more personal experience on Instagram.

Use hashtags If you know your audience then you will know what hashtags they will be searching for. Hashtags are a great way to find your audience and also by adding hastags to your images you can help your audience find you. You can add up to thirty hashtags.

Follow Follow Follow Just like Twitter, the more people you follow the more will follow you back. If you engage by liking and commenting you will draw them back to you and also put you in front of other followers who may come and check out your profile. To find your target audience think about where they are now on Instagram and who they are likely to be already following, go to those profiles and then follow them and start to engage with their content.

Interact and engage Interacting and commenting is very important on Instagram. Liking and commenting on photos not only helps you to build relationships but also helps you to get seen by other followers and you will find this makes a big difference to the number of people who start following you.

Responding to comments One of the most important things you can do is to responding to your followers by replying to their comments.

Embed Instagram photos or video in your website or blog You can tempt your website visitors and embed your most popular images on your website or blog. Simply visit your profile on the web and click on your photo and then on the three dots icon on the right of the photo to get the embed code.

Following influencers in your niche Building relationships with key influencers in your niche is invaluable. Not only can you learn from their content but also these people can have literally 1000's of followers, imagine if they follow you back and then share your content.

Advertising on Instagram Instagram is slowly rolling out its advertising with sponsored posts in the newsfeed. Advertising is available to a small number of brands in the US and is being rolled out slowly to get it right for both partners and the Instagram community as a whole. You can see if a post is sponsored as it will have the word 'sponsored' on the top right.

HOSTING AN INSTAGRAM PHOTO CONTEST

Photo contests are a great way to promote your brand, gain new followers, build your opt-in list, promote a new product and overall increase your reach on Instagram. Once you have decided what exactly you want to achieve with your contest you can get started very easily. Here are the steps you need to take to create your contest:

Choose a really good prize

You need to make sure your prize is specific to your brand in order to attract your target audience. If you are launching a new product then offering this as a prize is a great way to promote it. Gift cards can work very well as prizes especially if you have a wide range of products. A gift card for your competition will tend to appeal to a wider segment of your target audience.

Decide on the type of contest and the duration

You will need to decide what type of contest you wish to run, this can be anything from a simple sweepstake to a photo or video contest. It's a good idea to check out other contests for ideas, to do this simply search contest and competition hashtags on Instagram. If you decide to go with a photo or video contest you will need to decide on a theme, what sort of image or video you want your followers to upload and what your conditions are for entering. Asking your entrants to snap a picture of them using, eating or drinking your product is great way to promote your product. Try to keep it simple and put as few constraints as possible in order to encourage more followers to submit their photos.

The duration of your contest will depend very much on the type of contest. If you are asking your audience to submit videos you will need to give them longer to prepare than a simple sweepstake.

Choose a unique #hashtag

Hashtags make it really easy for you to collect your entrants photos around a particular subject and also help you to build a community around that hashtag so everyone can view the images relating to that hashtag. You will need to choose a #hashtag which is simple but unique to your brand so that it is less likely to be chosen by anyone else.

Create a landing page with entry rules

Create a page for your contest where followers can view results and simple rules. Remember to include the following:

Rules

Here are some guidelines for your contest rules:
- The dates that your contest is running and how and when the winner will be picked.
- That they must follow you on Instagram.
- That they must upload a photo relevant to the topic.
- How many photos they are allowed to upload.
- How many times they are allowed to enter.
- Who can enter. Is your contest limited to a particular country only?
- Where, when and how the winner will be announces.

Entry form

If you want to build your opt-in list then you will need your entrants to enter their email and their Instagram user name. There are third parties like www.wishpond.com and www.woobox.com who can administer your competitions. Using third parties can also make your contests look extremely professional and can take away the admin headache.

Create a graphic

You will need to create a compelling graphic with an attention grabbing headline. An image of the prize you are offering with brief details on how to enter can work very well. Remember the images on Instagram are small so any text like Hashtags, username or URL's have to be large enough. If you are creating a separate landing page for your contest then using a URL shortener like bit.ly can make it much easier for your contestants to remember and type in your landing page URL.

Make sure you add your entry details to the caption area of your post and add hashtags like #instagramcontest, #contest, #win, #competition so you can get found by more people searching for contests.

Once you have created your graphic you can also post it on other networks like Facebook, Twitter, Pinterest.

Promoting your contest

To get the word out about your contest you can add a banner to your business website and post your contest graphic on other social networks. You can also mail details of your contest to your email subscribers and add your contest details to contest websites that will let you submit your contest for free.

Sharing photos which have been submitted on other platforms not only gets the words out about your contest but also makes your followers feel rewarded. You can monitor all the posts being uploaded with a tool called statigram.

Post Contest

After the contest make sure you announce the winner and share on your other platforms too. Also ask the winner if they can upload a picture of them using /eating /enjoying their prize or you could create a video of them receiving their prize.

Now is the time to mail your entrants and try and convert them into customers, offering them a discount voucher is also a very good idea to help them feel rewarded for entering.

Advertising on Instagram

Instagram is slowly rolling out its advertising with sponsored posts in the newsfeed. Advertising is available to a small number of brands in the US and is being started slowly to get it right for both partners and the Instagram community as a whole.

ADVERTISING ON INSTAGRAM

With over 400 million users, Instagram is now a serious contender for businesses and brands to spend their advertising dollars. Up until now brands have found it difficult to drive traffic to their website as there has been nowhere to add a URL to an individual post. This has been a huge frustration for businesses, the only place you could add a URL was to your Bio or the Geo Tag field which is not clickable.

For some time I have been wondering how Instagram were planning to monetize their platform. It turned out that the best solution was the simplest and Instagram's easy fix was to add a clickable link to advertiser's posts. So now if you advertise on Instagram you can effectively drive traffic directly to your website.

Instagram Ad's are now available to businesses large and small and once you know how, it's as easy as 123 . You can now advertise to more of their target audience and with the call to action buttons you can direct their audience to where ever you like on the web. What better way to visually promote your product to your target audience than with a beautiful image.

It takes a while to familiarise yourself and navigate around the Power Editor but this tutorial will save you loads of time.

1. Firstly, if you have not already got an account with Facebook and Instagram then you will need accounts on both platforms.

2. If you already have an Instagram account then you need to link it to Facebook. Go to **Settings** on your Facebook page and then click on **Instagram Adverts** and follow the steps to link your account

3. Next go to Facebook's Power Editor https://www.facebook.com/ads/manage/powereditor and go to **Manage Adverts**

4. Next under Choose a campaign click **Create New** add your campaign name

5. Now select the Buying Type, **Auction**

6. Then Choose your objective. With Instagram Ads you can choose out of 3

- Clicks to Website

- Mobile App Installs

- Video Views

7. Then under **Choose an Advert Set** select **Create New and name your advert set.**

8. Under **Create New Advert** add the name of your Advert and click **Create** at the bottom.

9. Next Click of **Advert Set** then tick the Advert set box and then the pencil icon.

You will then arrive at the section where you set your budget, schedule your adverts ,choose your audience, choose where you want your advert to appear (this is where you select Instagram)

- **Budget** You can select either daily budget or a weekly budget.
- **Schedule** This is where you schedule your advert start and end time or you can run as ongoing. If you are running a lifetime budget you can let your adverts run all the time.
- **Audience** (see below for image) You can select a **new audience** or choose a **custom audience or App Activity** (people who have taken a certain action on your app) . If you select a **custom audience** you can choose from a **Customer List, Website traffic (** A list of people who have visited your website, to do this you need to install the Facebook pixel on your website) If you are choosing a **new audience** then you can select your **Location, Demographics (Age, Gender, Relationship, Education, Work, Home. Ethnic Affinity, Generation, Parent, Politics, Life Events) and then you can choose your connections** (how people are connected to you through a page, app or event) **language, Interests and behaviour.**
- **Placement** Next you choose your placement, this is where you choose **Instagram** and then **All Mobile Devices**. If you were advertising on Facebook this is where you would choose where you wanted your advert in the Desktop or Mobile Newsfeed.
- **Optimization & Pricing** Next you choose how you want your advert optimised **Link clicks to website/Pay per impressions** is recommended.
- **Advanced Delivery.** You can choose from **Standard or Accelerated (show your adverts as quickly as possible)**

10. Once you have selected all your options you can create your advert. Click the **Advert Icon**. Tick the Advert and click on the pencil icon.

11. You will need to select the URL you want your people to go to and then add the text for your advert. You can only add up to 300 characters and you can include hashtags in this text here if you like.

12. You can then select whether you want to add an image or video. With an image you image size should be ideally 1080 × 1080 pixels and as with Facebook you are not allowed to include more than 20 % text. make sure you add a really beautiful attention grabbing image. You can crop your image in the power editor too. The recommended format for a video add is mp4 or .mov with at least a 720 resolution and the maximum length of your video should be not more than 30 seconds. Here are Facebook's Guidelines for ads, it's definitely worth reading [Click Here for Facebook's Advert Policy]

13. You can then add a call to action Apply Now, Book Now, Contact Us, Download, Learn More, Shop Now, Sign Up , Watch More. You can also add your own call to action, for example Take a selfie, tag a friend/ your friends or sign up to a newsletter.

14. You can track your URL by adding URL Tags and Facebook's Tracking pixel to your Website.

15. Lastly you need to cheque all your setting, review your changes by clicking the big green button on the top right and then submit your advert for review.

16. To get the most out of your campaign it's a good idea to test a few Ad's by either using different images and text or choosing a different audience within your target audience. For example, you could choose different demographics for the advert or select different interests or behaviours.

CHAPTER SIX

DAY TO DAY ACTIVITY

THERE ARE CERTAIN things that you will need to do on a day to day basis to run your campaign on Instagram. It is a good idea to allot a specific amount of time and a particular time of the day to do this. Here are some of the things you will need to do:

Following your followers

This is important if you are customers are business owners themselves. Following your prospects and customers will go a long way in building relationships. By following you are showing them that you are interested in what they have to say and also helping them to achieve their goals by helping to build their audience.

Engaging, commenting and replying

When your followers start to engage with your content make sure you are listening and responding to them. Everyone is aiming for shares, likes and comments so if you are helping others out by commenting and liking their content it is going to draw attention to your brand and they are more likely to take interest in your content. This is one area where the reciprocation rule works very well on Instagram. Engaging with content will also draw attention to you and your brand and you will find that people will click on your page or profile to find out who you are and you may very well end up with another follower. Be friendly to your audience, be chatty, authentic, genuine and embrace the conversation. All this will all go a long well in building a positive image for your brand and will set you apart from your others who are continually ambushing their audience with self promotion.

Showing your audience you value and respect them

If you value and respect your audience they will most probably love, respect and value your business. Be kind, generous, offer as much help and value as possible, reply to their comments and make it obvious that you value your audience and are listening to them. Don't be afraid to be yourself rather than a stiff brand with no personality.

Dealing with negative comments

Every business at some time will have to deal with negativity from followers. Hopefully if you have a good product then this is not going to happen too often. There are 'trolls' out there who have nothing better to do than post negative comments, the best thing to do with them is just ignore them, delete their comments and block them if you have to.

However there will be real customers who have real concerns and complaints and may post negative comments publicly, there may also be people who really want to lash out to gain your attention as quickly as possible and spread the news to their friends too!

You need to deal with complaints as quickly as possible and be as transparent and authentic as possible. The best thing to do is to apologise and say how sorry you are to hear of the inconvenience they have been caused and offer to continue the conversation and deal with their concern by asking to call you or email you. You can then deal with this privately, give your customer the full attention they deserve and decide on your next course of action or compensation.

CHAPTER SEVEN

MEASURING AND MONITORING YOUR RESULTS ON INSTAGRAM

TRACKING YOUR RESULTS on Instagram is the best way to find out if you are reaching the right audience and uploading the right content on Instagram.

Tracking your results is harder with Instagram. Since you cannot add clickable links in captions it's more difficult to drive traffic to particular web pages. Brands can analyze their success by measuring the number of likes, comments and also their overall reach.

Having a large number of followers is important but engagement rates are more important. Once you see which images are creating the most engagement you can try to produce more of the same. Filters can make a difference to the engagement too, so make sure your keep a track of which ones are working for you. Once you know which are your favorite filters you can organize into order of importance on the app, this will save you heaps of time.

Measuring and monitoring your results and performance against your original goals and objectives on an ongoing basis is essential. This is where many businesses go wrong by carrying on aimlessly with what they are doing instead of checking to see what is working and what is not. Once you have this information you can steer your campaign in the right direction and achieve the results you are looking for.

Once you get started you'll probably need to adjust your objectives according to how you are performing. For example, you may need to follow more people in order to grow the number of your followers or you may need to post images more often to drive more traffic to your blog or website.

GOOGLE ANALYTICS

The Overview Report

This report lets you see at a glance how much conversion value is generated from social channels. It compares all conversions with those resulting from social.

The Conversions Report

The Conversions Report helps you to quantify the value of social and shows conversion rates and the monetary value of conversions that occurred due to referrals from Instagram and any of the other social networks. Google Analytics can link visits from Instagram with the goals you have chosen and your E - commerce transactions. To do this you will need to configure your goals in Google Analytics which is found under 'Admin' and then 'Goals'. Goals in Google Analytics allow you to measure how often visitors take or complete a specific action and you can either create goals from the templates offered or create your own custom goals. The Conversions report can be found in the Standard Reporting tab under Traffic Sources > Social > Conversions.

The Networks Referral Report

The Networks Referral report tells you how many visitors the social networks have referred to your website and shows you how many page views, visits, the duration of the visits and the average number of pages viewed per visit. From this information you can determine which network referred the highest quality of traffic.

Data Hub Activity Report

The Data Hub activity report shows how people are engaging with your site on the social networks. You can see the most recent URLs that were shared, how they were shared and what was said.

The Social Visitors Flow Report
This report shows you the initial paths that your visitors took from social sites through your site and where they exited.

The Landing Pages Report
This report shows you engagement metrics for each URL. These include page views, average visit duration and pageviews and pages viewed per visit.

The Trackback Report The Trackback report shows you which sites are linking to your content and how many visits those sites are sending to you. This can help you to work out which sort of content is the most successful so you can create similar and also helps you to build relationships with those who are constantly linking to your content.

THIRD PARTY APPLICATIONS
There are free tools that are available to help measure and analyze your campaigns such as:

Statigram
This is a tool solely for Instagram and provides statistics for the number of images you have, the number of likes, comments and followers.

It shows you which of your pages have the highest engagement, which of your followers are the most engaged and your growth or loss of followers. You can also manage contests with this tool.

Nitrogram
This tool shows engagement rates, statistics per photo, follower count and number of images shared. You can follow all the posts on #hashtags related to your brand and identify your biggest advocates. You can also

view the top brands on Instagram.

Sumall

Sumall is definitely an analytics tool to keep an eye on as it can track all your campaigns on all your platforms. You can track sales, site visits and followers all in one place.

CHAPTER EIGHT

BUILDING YOUR BRAND THROUGH INSTAGRAM

YOUR MAIN AIM through this whole process is going to be to connect, capture, and convert your prospects through your website or blog, Facebook, and through other social networks, and this involves the following:

- **Connect:** Your product needs to be the connection between your prospect and what they need so the first thing you need to do is connect those two things. In order to do this you need to identify who they are, find them out of all the millions of people on the Internet, and then connect with them by offering them something they want or need.

- **Capture:** Once you have found them you need to capture them on your website, blog, Instagram, or any other social media platforms. This is so you can continue your relationship with them either by email or through Instagram and continue to communicate your brand message. To do this you need to offer them some sort of incentive so you can capture their name and email address.

- **Convert:** When you have captured your prospect you need to convert them into a paying customer by nurturing them and continuing to build a relationship by offering them the content they want through email and Instagram and then moving them toward signing up for a special or exclusive offer.

To achieve this successfully you are going to need to have a well-defined brand, and that brand needs to be communicated through everything you do or say through Instagram, your website, blog, and your email campaign.

Whether you are a one person small business, a large corporation, or an organization, your brand is one of the most important attributes of your business. Your brand is what you want your prospects and customers to respect, trust, and fall in love with so they will buy and continue to buy your products and services. Your brand is what is going to set you apart from any other business and what will give your business the competitive edge.

Never has there been a better time for your business to build your brand and communicate your brand message to your target audience than through Instagram. Your brand is the main ingredient for success, and Instagram is giving you the channel to visually communicate it. You can literally communicate with your audience every day. If you get it right and connect the right brand experience with the right target audience, you are onto an all-around winner.

It may be that you have a well-established brand already or maybe you have not created your brand yet or it just needs some tweaking or fine tuning. Maybe you are not exactly sure what your brand is, or maybe you feel it needs a complete overhaul. Whatever your situation is, you need to know that your brand is going to underpin your whole Instagram campaign, and it needs to be strong, clear, well-defined, and consistent. Once defined, your business is going to create it, be it, communicate it, display it, picture it, speak it, promote it, and most of all, be true to it. This chapter is going to take you through everything you need know and do to define and create your brand so you can get into the hearts and minds of your target audience by communicating the right message and brand experience.

There are many definitions of the word brand but this is the one I like best because it incorporates pretty much all the necessary information you will need to help you to define your own brand.

Brand, the definition

Your brand is more than a name, symbol, or logo. It is your commitment and your promise to your customer. Your brand is the defined personality of either yourself as an individual brand or your product, service, company, or organization. It's what sets you apart and differentiates your business from your competition and any other business. Your brand is created and influenced by your vision and everything you stand for, including people, visuals, culture, style, perception, words, messages, PR, opinions, news media, and, especially, social media.

Why is your brand so important to your business?

Branding is important because it helps you and your business build and create powerful and lasting relationships by communicating everything you want to say about your product or service to your prospects and customers. A strong brand encourages loyalty and will ultimately create a strong customer base and increase your sales by doing the following:

- Demonstrating to your prospects and customers that you are professional and committed to offering them what you promise
- Making your business easily recognizable
- Creating a clear distinction from your competition
- Making your business memorable
- Creating an emotional attachment with your audience
- Helping to create trust
- Helping to build customer loyalty and repeat custom
- Creating a valuable asset which will be financially beneficial if you sell your business
- Creating a competitive advantage

To do all the above you are going to have to find a way to get into the hearts and minds of your customers so they will ultimately buy and continue to buy your products or services. Before launching your campaign and setting up profiles, posting content, and engaging, you will need to have a clear picture of exactly what your brand is or what you want your brand to be. You will need to define exactly how your brand is perceived now, how you want your brand to be perceived, where your business fits into the market, who your target audience is, and how you want your business to develop in the future.

To do this you need a deep understanding of your business and the people who are going to be most interested in your products and how you are going to serve them. When it comes to defining your ideal target audience, you need to work out which of your products are the most popular and which are the most profitable so you can focus your efforts in finding and connecting with the right audience and then creating the right brand experience for them.

YOUR VISION/YOUR STORY

If you want to create a strong brand, one of the first things you need to do is create a clear visual picture of how you see your business now and in the future. This is about daring to see what your business could be without constraints or limitations.

This exercise will not only help you to work out what you want to achieve financially and creatively, but it also makes you focus on what really matters and will help you to create your own unique voice and story. This is incredibly important when it comes to your branding as this is what is going to make your business stand out from others and give you that edge.

To do this, you need to get away from all distractions and think about how you would like to see your business grow and develop in the next three years. This is more than just putting a mission statement together. This is about your core business beliefs, why you are doing it, what you want your business to be, and how you want to be perceived in your market. To help you do this you will need to ask yourself the following questions and record your answers:

- Why did you originally start your business or why are you starting a business?
- How did your original business idea come about?
- What changes are you looking to make in peoples' lives?
- What are you hoping to achieve?
- What aspects of your business are really important to you?
- What are your hopes and dreams?
- What is your definition of success?
- What sort of turnover and income defines that success?
- How many employees does your business have?
- Why are you in business?
- What are your core values in your business?
- What impact do you want to have?
- What influence do you want to have?
- What sort of things do you want the media to be saying about you?
- What do you want your customers to be saying about you?
- How you want to be portrayed on social media?
- How many Instagram folewers do you want?
- What markets are you in? Are you local, national, or international?

Once you have completed this exercise, you will have all the material you need so that you can create the unique experience required to make your business stand out from all the others in your niche. This is the first step toward creating a brand for your business. This is the beginning of your story.

DEFINING YOUR BRAND

Whether you are responsible for defining, creating, and developing your brand in-house or you are employing a local branding and marketing agency, you will need to carry out an analysis of your business to define your brand. Completing the following exercise will help you to define and find clarity about your brand:

- A factual description of what your business is and the purpose of your business.
- Describe your product or service in one sentence.
- List all your products and/or services.
- What are the benefits and features of all of your products?
- Which are your most profitable products/services?
- Which are your most popular products/services?
- Who are your ideal customers for each of your products or services? (Consumer or business, age, gender, income, occupation, education, stage in family life cycle.)
- Out of these customers, who are the ones who are most likely to buy your most profitable products?
- Is the market and demand large enough to provide you with the number of customers you need to buy your most profitable products and achieve your financial goals?
- If your answer to the previous question is no then ask yourself the same question for each of your other products.
- Who are your three main competitors? (Have a look at their Instagram account.)
- What distinguishes your business from your competition? What special thing are you bringing to the market that is of real value? What is your unique selling point? What solutions are your products offering your customers that will meet their needs or solve their problems?
- If you are already in business, then write down what your customers are already saying about your business. What do you think they would say about how your product or service makes them feel emotionally? (You may need to ask your customers if you do not already know.) What qualities and words would you use to describe the personality of your business as it is now? Here

are some examples of words you may wish to use: high cost, low cost, high quality, value for money, expensive, cheap, excellent customer service, friendly, professional, happy, serious, innovative, eccentric, quiet, loud, beautiful, relaxing, motivating, sincere, adventurous, amusing, charming, decisive, kind, imaginative, proactive, intuitive, loving, trustworthy, extrovert, vibrant, transparent, intelligent, creative, dynamic, resourceful.

- Now, whether you are already in business or starting out, write down all the words to describe how you want and need your brand to be perceived and what qualities you want to be associated with your brand in order to match the needs and expectations of your ideal customers. If you are already in business, hopefully this will be exactly the same from how you perceive you are at the current time.

- What is the evidence that backs up what you have said about your brand? This could be customer testimonials or any evidence about product or service quality.

- What is the biggest opportunity for your business right now?

- What products are you thinking of introducing in the near future?

HOW TO GET INTO THE HEARTS AND MINDS OF YOUR TARGET AUDIENCE

Your target audience is your most important commodity, as they are the future customers and ambassadors of your business. Every single one of them is valuable, and every single one of them can make a difference to your business. This can be because they are actually going to buy your products or simply spread the word by interacting with you on Instagram.

However, it's a big social world out there. The possibilities of finding new people are limitless, but targeting everyone is not the solution. The biggest mistake you can make is trying to reach everyone and then not appealing to anyone. Your first step is to identify exactly who the people are who are going to be interested in your products or services, and then you need to find out everything about them. You need to get inside their heads and work out what motivates these people, what they are interested in, what their needs, hopes, aspirations, and fears are, and what are their dreams. Your product or service is the link between them and what they want. When you know this you can tailor every single message or piece of content toward them.

When you know exactly who your ideal customers are, Instagram offers you the opportunity to go and find and reach them. It's then up to you to capture them so you can continue to communicate with them. When you know everything about your customers you are more likely to speak the right language to be able to communicate with them and build trust to the point where the next natural progression is for them to buy your product.

It's only when you truly understand your audience that you can start converting them into customers. Once you know you are targeting the right audience, you can confidently focus every ounce of your effort creating exactly the right content, nurturing them, engaging with them, and looking after them. It's only a matter of time before they will buy your product.

Creating your ideal customer persona or avatar

The following exercise is absolutely essential. Your answers to the questions will be the very information that is going to help you communicate with your customer in the right way, by providing them with the right content and the correct brand experience. Once you have done this exercise you are going to own some very powerful information. If you do not do this exercise it is very unlikely that you are going to be able to truly connect with your target audience in the way that is necessary to build trust so that you can ultimately convert them into your customers.

Your answers to the questions in the previous section will have given you a clear idea of which types of customers you need to target to give you the best chance of achieving your financial goals. You now need to find out everything about them so you can get your brand into their hearts and minds. The best way to do this is to create an imaginary persona or avatar of your ideal customer and you can build this picture by finding out the following:

- Describe your ideal customer and include the following details: are they a consumer or in business, their age, gender, income, occupation, education, and stage in family life cycle.
- Where do they live?
- What do they want most of all?
- What are their core values?
- What is their preferred lifestyle?
- What do they do on a day-to-day basis?
- What are their hopes and aspirations?
- What important truth matters to them?
- What motivates and inspires them?
- What sort of routines do they have?
- What are their day-to-day priorities?
- How do they have fun?
- What do they do in their spare time?
- What subjects are they interested in?
- Which books do they read?
- Which TV programs do they watch?
- What magazines do they read?
- Who do they follow on social media?
- Who are their role models?
- What really makes them tick?
- What are their fears and frustrations?
- What are their suspicions?
- What are their insecurities?
- What are their typical worries?

- What is the perfect solution to their worries?
- What are their dreams?
- What do they need to make them feel happy and fulfilled?

Big Questions

To answer the following questions you will need to step inside your ideal customer's mind and imagine you are them.

- How do you feel when you find your product or service? What is your initial emotional reaction?
- What are the words that go through your head?
- How can I justify buying this product for myself?
- Are you ready to buy immediately?
- Do you have any suspicions that the product may not be what it says?
- What are those suspicions? Why do you have them?
- Do you need more convincing?
- What do you need to convince you that the product is right for you?
- What do you feel when you have the product in your hand?

The reason why these are such big questions is because your answers to them will establish whether or not you have correctly defined your ideal customer and whether you have really understood their needs, desires, and fears. If you are imagining yourself as your ideal customer and you are saying "woo-hoo", ecstatically jumping up and down with glee, immediately buying the product, or relieved that you have at long last found the solution to your problem, then you have created the right avatar. If not, then you need to think again.

It's only when you have imagined yourself in the hearts and minds of your target audience that you are going to be able to connect with them on any emotional level. With the information from the above exercise, you will have everything you need to produce exactly the right content to match the needs, desires, and expectations of your ideal customer so that you can create the right brand experience and sell your products. This information is like gold.

COMMUNICATING YOUR BRAND

Once you have gone through all the processes outlined in this chapter you will have a clear idea about what your brand is, what is stands for, and how you stand out from similar businesses. You now have to work out how to best communicate this to your ideal customer so that when they hear or see your brand name they immediately make that essential emotional connection. This is what is going to make them eventually love remember your brand above all others.

When you are clear about what your brand is, what it stands for, and how you are going to stand out from other similar businesses, you then need to work out how you can communicate this message in the best possible way. Your main aim here is to create an emotional connection with your target audience that is going to help them grow to love your brand, remember your brand, and remain loyal to it. To do this you need to communicate your brand story through every aspect of your business, including your social media campaign.

With the information you now have you are armed with everything you need to create a consistent brand. If you have not already done so, you can either hand all this information over to a marketing agency or use it yourself to create all the following:

- **Your logo:** Your logo will give a clear guideline for all your promotional material, including your website or blog, stationery, templates, or any marketing material that needs to be created for online or offline promotion.
- **Your brand message: This is** the main message you want to communicate about your brand.
- **Your tagline:** A short, memorable statement about your brand

that captures the personality of your brand and communicates how you or your product will benefit your customer.

- **All your 'about' descriptions:** You can communicate your brand story through all your 'about' sections on all your social media platforms you are using.

- **The content you create for your business:** Every piece of content you create for your business needs to be tailor-made for your target audience. You will need to pick who and what subjects or topics you want to be associated with your brand, as anything you pick to write about will be a representation of your brand.

- **Your website and/or blog:** The 'about' page of your website is probably the most visited page of any website and there is a reason for this. People want to find out about your business and they want to find out what is different or special about it. This is a great place to introduce and expand on the story of your brand. This is where you can really go to town and communicate your beliefs and how you are unique. Also, the visual style of your website or blog and your unique voice should be evident throughout your site and be consistent with your brand.

- **Video content:** Videos are an incredibly powerful way of creating a personal connection with your audience. Make sure that whatever video content you produce and whatever you say is always consistent with your brand.

CHAPTER NINE

THE ESSENTIAL INSTAGRAM MARKETING PLAN

BEFORE LAUNCHING INTO your campaign you will need to know exactly what you want your business to achieve and what you want to achieve through marketing your business on Instagram. Without the necessary planning and preparation, your campaign is very unlikely to succeed.

The next few chapters take you through everything you need to do to plan your campaign before actually posting content. In this chapter you will learn how to create your mission statement, set goals and objectives, and plan the strategies and tactics you need to implement to achieve those goals. In the following chapter you will learn exactly how to prepare your business, your website and blog, and your email campaign so you can capture and convert.

CREATING YOUR MISSION STATEMENT

Many campaigns fail at the first hurdle simply because they do not have a clear idea about why they are undertaking in a campaign or what they want to achieve. They set up a Instagram account and have little or no idea why exactly they are doing it. "Everyone else is doing it ... we probably should too." Then they launch in without first articulating the purpose of their Instagram campaign and aimlessly start posting content. Before long, they realize that this is having no positive effect on their business, and they either give up or continue half-heartedly.

Once you have defined your brand and your target audience you will need to produce your mission statement for your social media campaign. Your mission statement is vital for your business as a whole and for your prospects and customers, and it should clearly state your commitment and promise to them as well as communicating your brand message. You will be able to include this in your Instagram bio. To create your mission statement, simply follow these for four easy steps:

- **Describe what your business does:** Describe exactly what you do, what you offer, and the purpose of your business.
- **Describe the way you operate:** Include your core values, your level of customer service, and your commitment to your customers. You can include how your core values contribute to the quality of your product or service.
- **Who are you doing it for?:** Who are your customers? Business owners, entrepreneurs, working women, gardeners, shop owners, etc.
- **The value you are bringing:** What benefit are you offering your customers ? What value are you bringing them?

Once you have created your statement, everyone will know exactly what you are about. You will know exactly what you need to deliver to your customers. Your employees will know what is expected of them. Your customers and prospects will know exactly what your promise is and what they can expect when buying your products and services.

SETTING YOUR GOALS AND OBJECTIVES

Setting goals and objectives is the key to your success on Instagram. Once they are set you will be ready to plan and create the strategies and tactics to achieve those goals and objectives and you will be able to review and measure the success of your campaign.

Definition of a goal

A goal is a statement rooted in your business's mission and it will define what you want to accomplish and offer a broad direction for your business to follow. The three main goals of any business will ultimately be to increase sales, to reduce costs and to improve customer service and each goal will have a direct effect on the others. Here are some examples of goals and objectives within those three main goals:

1. To increase revenue and generate sales

- To increase website traffic.
- To increase brand awareness through Instagram.
- To build a reputation as an expert within the industry.
- To build a loyal and engaged community on Instagram.
- To increase the number of customers from word of mouth and referrals.
- To increase the number of sales.
- To increase average spend per customer.
- To increase the number of leads generated.
- To introduce new products.
- To increase online visibility.
- To promote an event.
- To build a highly targeted list of email subscribers.
- To connect with new customers.
- To build trust and build relationships with prospects and customers.
- To put a content marketing strategy in place.
- To increase business in 'X' country/state.
- To become a thought leader in your industry.
- To develop new markets by introducing product into 'X' country/state.
- To decrease spend on traditional forms of advertising and invest 'X' amount in Instagram marketing.
- To build relationships with key influencers on Instagram.

2. To reduce Costs

- To decrease spend on traditional forms of advertising and invest in Instagram. marketing.

3. To deliver customer satisfaction and retain customers

- To answer customer questions promptly.
- To respond to customer complaints promptly, politely and helpfully.
- To provide online help/technical support.
- To respond to customer feedback.
- To listen to your customers.

Setting measurable objectives

Once you set your broader goals then you need to get more specific and create SMART objectives (specific, measurable, attainable, relevant and time bound). Here is an explanation of exactly what each of those terms means:

- **Specific** You need to target particular areas for improvement.
- **Measurable** Your progress needs to be quantifiable and putting concrete figures on your goals is essential for success and is the only way to measure the effectiveness of your campaign.
- **Attainable / Realistic** You need to be realistic with the resources you have available and the results you are expecting need to be realistic.
- **Relevant** Your goals need to be relevant to the business climate you are in.
- **Time Bound** Make sure you set a realistic time period to achieve your goals. If a time is not set then things don't tend to get done.

Here are some examples of the sort of SMART objectives you should be setting:

- To Increase sales of product 'X' by X%
- To build an audience of 'X' number followers on **Instagram** within one year.
- To increase number of followers by 'X' per week.

- To increase website traffic from **Instagram** by 'X' times.
- To increase opt-in list subscribers by 'X' number per week
- To Increase conversions from **Instagram** by 'X' per week.
- To increase the number of leads generated from **Instagram** by 'X' per week.
- To increase the number of new customers by 'X' per month.
- To increase the average spend per customer by 'X'.
- Introduce X number of new products every 6 months.
- To increase sales from X country/state by 'X'%
- To decrease spend on traditional forms of advertising by 'X' and invest 'X' amount in **Instagram** marketing.

CHOOSING YOUR STATEGIES AND TACTICS

Once you have set your quantifiable goals and objectives you are going to have to work out how you are going to accomplish them using Instagram. You will need to think about the strategies and tactics you are going to use and they need to be quantifiable as well. Here are some examples of the strategies you may want to implement:

- To post images on Instagram 'X' times per day/week.
- To post 'X' number of videos per day/week/month.
- To follow 'X' number of new accounts a day/week.
- To create 'X' number of blog posts per week/month and post them on Instagram with images.
- To post 'X' number of offers per month/6 months on Instagram.
- To run 'X' competitions/contests per year on Instagram.
- To spend 'X' minutes per day liking and commenting on followers images.
- To follow 'X' number of influencers on Instagram per week.

Of course at the beginning you are going to need to make an educated guess at the number of times you are going to need to do one thing to achieve another. As your campaign runs you will need to adjust certain aspects to achieve what you set out to achieve. For example, you may need to spend more time following people in order to increase the number of your followers you have, you may need to change the type of images you are posting to increase the amount of engagement.

The only way you can do this is by constantly monitoring and measuring your results against the original goals and objectives you set and adjusting your campaign accordingly.

CREATING YOUR INSTAGRAM POSTING CALENDAR

Now that you have your strategies in place, you will have a good idea of the amount and type of content you need to post to achieve those objectives. One of the most challenging tasks of your Instagram campaign is going to be to consistently deliver a high standard of content to your followers on a daily basis. You are going to need to post between one to four times a day. This does not mean you need to create numerous blog articles each day, but you are going to need to communicate in some way and find unique ways for your audience to interact with your brand and offer some kind of value on a regular basis. This may seem daunting to begin with, but you will be surprised just how one idea leads to another.

To help you map out your content for the next six months or the year ahead, you need to create a Instagram posting calendar which is going to be your key to consistent posting. There are many online tools and apps that can help you with this. Google Calendar is a very good calendar to use, and it lets you color code the different types of posts. You can also use Hootsuite, the social media dashboard, to plot out your calendar or use a spreadsheet in Excel. There are also other online applications, like www.trello.com, which has easy to use drag-and-drop features. Using mind-mapping applications like 'Simplemind' can really help when brainstorming for content ideas.

To get started you will simply need to map out and schedule the days of the week for each week of the year and decide what types of post you are going to create for certain days. You will need to balance the type of content in order to create variety and interest for your audience. You then need to create topics or themes and then break the year down into weeks/months and make a schedule. You can then add all the things that you are planning within your business, like offers, contests, product launches, and webinars, and then add all the things going on outside your business, like public holidays and special events. You then need to incorporate all that information into your daily action plan.

It may seem daunting to look at a blank calendar, but you will be surprised how it comes together when you start breaking it down into months, weeks, and days. A posting calendar will help you keep your campaign focused, on track, and in line with your brand and your marketing goals and also keep it balanced in terms of the subject and type of media you use. A calendar will help you look ahead and help you to incorporate your marketing plan into your Instagram campaign. It may be that you are launching a new product, or maybe certain products tie in with specific holidays. You may have certain industry events you need to attend or are perhaps creating your own. Maybe you are going to run a competition at a certain time of the year. Whatever it is you are planning throughout the year, you need to include it on your calendar.

Managing your Instagram Account

Spreesy.com

Spreesy is a service which enables selling directly on Instagram. Anyone can purchase products by commenting on your Instagram posts with their email address. Comment buying is a very popular way to purchase and customers can comment with their email address on any stoppable post and then are sent a secure link to purchase the item.

Paywithpenny.com

This app lets you sell items directly over Instagram with a hashtag. The seller posts items to Instagram, the buyer comments sold and

PayWithPenny takes care of the rest.

Iconosquare (formerly Statigram)
Oconisquare is incredibly useful for brands, it's a free app that helps you to manage your account and host contests on Instagram. You can view and manage comments chronologically and you can reply easily to comments without having to add the username every time and you can do this from your desktop or laptop.

You can also organize your followers into groups of followers. This way when visit the feed on Iconisquare you can select the group you want to view. This helps to cut out the noise and lets you see posts from users you are particularly interested in. Simply visit the app and then sign in with Instagram and go to your followings tab, you can then click on users and underneath add your group names and then add users to the groups.

Iconisquare also shows statistics for your account and shows you your follower growth, engagement rates and also show you which followers you are losing. You can also view your most commented and liked posts and also there is a graph which shows you when you receive most on your interactions. It's all incredibly useful information.

Instacommenter
Instacommenter is an app that lets you keep track of your who you have replied to and who you have not replied to.

Instafollow and unfollowgram
Instafollow and Unfollowgram are apps that let you see who followed and unfollowed you and let you unfollow users easily.

Repost for Instagram
This and other similar apps let you repost photos from other users profiles while giving credit to the original Instagrammer by adding a strip to the bottom top or side of the image.

Hootsuite

Hootsuite now allows you to add your Instagram posts to Hootsuite and then schedule your post. Hootsuite will not automatically post the update to Instagram but will send you a notification to remind you to post the update.

Latergramme.me

Later gramme is another application which will allow you to post your update and then remind you to post the update at the scheduled time. This means you can plan and post on the fly.

Chapter Ten

Preparing your Business for Success

WHETHER YOUR SITE is being found through an organic search, an advertising campaign, Instagram, or any other social media platform, all your hard work is going to be wasted unless you have put a system in place to capture leads and convert them into customers. This system has to start from the moment your prospect either hits your website, your blog, or your Instagram profile, and your ultimate goal is to convert your browsers into buyers.

Firstly, the unfortunate fact is that the majority of your website visitors are unlikely to buy from you on their first visit. If you do not have a website that grabs their attention within the first couple of seconds, then they will move very quickly onto another site. Secondly, even if your site does catch their eye, they are still likely to check out other sites and still may not return. To make any kind of impact at all your site needs to grab their attention and then capture their email address so you can continue your relationship with them through email. This chapter is going to take you through steps you will need to take, from getting your website or blog ready to setting up and creating your email campaign.

Email is still one of the most powerful ways to convert prospects into customers and has a conversion rate three times higher than social media conversion rates. That is not to say that your Instagram campaign is any less important, as this is where you are going to find and nurture your leads and transfer them to your opt-in by either capturing them on Instagram or on your website or blog. This chapter is going to take you through steps you will need to take from getting your website or blog ready to setting up and creating your email campaign.

PREPARING YOUR WEBSITE FOR SUCCESS

Whether you already have a website or blog or you are creating a new site from scratch, you need to make sure it has the necessary features to grab the attention of your target audience and capture their email addresses. Capturing the email addresses of your target audience has to be one of your most important goals when creating your website. Once your prospects have voluntarily submitted their email address, you have the opportunity to build a relationship, communicate your message, and promote your products and services on an ongoing and regular basis. A well thought-out and crafted email campaign can immediately establish trust and favor with your subscribers. Don't forget that it is you who owns your opt-in list and nobody can take it away from you. As long as you are providing your subscribers value with great content, they are likely to want to keep hearing from you. Remember you cannot rely on social media to continue your relationship as these platforms are changing all the time. You need to build your email list.

Once you have completed the exercise in the branding section and have your ideal customer persona or avatar, you will have a clear picture of what your target audience's pain point or problem is and how your product can help solve their problem or make their life better in some way. If you have a blog, and most businesses today need a blog, you will also have all the tools you need to create the right content to attract your target audience. Armed with this information you are halfway ready to putting a system in place to sell, so your products sell themselves and your website is working like an extra sales person selling your products 24/7.

When your visitor arrives at your site, you have only three seconds to grab their attention. You need to connect emotionally with them and let them know immediately that they have arrived at the right place by communicating exactly how you are going to help them and what it is you are offering them.

Once they are on your site, you then need to win their interest and confidence so that they will voluntarily submit their email address. To do this you will need to create a lead magnet and offer your audience something which is incredibly valuable to them for free. There are numerous ways you can do this and which one you use will depend very much on what type of business you are and what your goals are. If you are a business offering technical solutions, then you could offer them a free trial. If you are offering information, then you could offer them a free report, a short video training series, or an ebook. If you are selling some kind of product or service, you could offer them a money-off voucher. These work particularly well for restaurants and the service industry as a whole. Whatever you are offering, it needs to be really good to attract your audience and get them to volunteer their email.

Here are the features you need to have on your website or blog or any landing page with a special offer.

- **Keep your design simple:** Your site needs to have a clean and simple design, and you need to communicate your most important message clearly and concisely to your target audience. Your most important content with any call-to-action needs to be placed above the fold, where they will be easily seen, and your call-to-action should have an easily seen button link rather than just a text link.
- **Make your site easy to navigate:** Really this is so important. Try to use the minimum number of pages you can and make your menu titles as easy to understand as possible.
- **Clearly communicate your message:** You want your visitors to subscribe to your opt-in, so you need to place your compelling offer with an image and title of the offer somewhere where it is visible. The message and benefit of your offer needs be descriptive and specific.

- **Add a clear call-to-action:** In order for your visitors to sign up, they will need to be told what to do. Make sure you have a direct call-to-action, for example, "Download your free ebook now" or "Sign up for your discount voucher now." Your call-to-action needs to be clearly visible with an eye-catching button link which is much more effective than a text link.

- **Add clear contact information:** Make it easy for your prospects to contact you by placing your contact details where they will be easily seen. With the technology available, you can even add chat features so that as soon as your prospect arrives on your site a chat form appears asking if you can be of any assistance. Obviously you need the resources to be able to man this, but it is an incredibly powerful way of quickly building trust and showing how much you value your website visitors by being available to answer any of their questions.

- **Email capture form:** Your email capture form needs to be as simple as possible, preferably just asking for their name and email. You need to state on the form that their email address is safe with you and will not be shared with anyone. Make sure your form is in a prominent position and consider using a pop-up form that appears after 20 seconds after your prospect has arrived on your site. Your email sign-up form needs to go at the top, side, and bottom of your webpage and also on your 'about page,' which is often the most popular page on your site.

- **Privacy policy:** You need a clear privacy policy on your website and to make it clear that you will not be spamming them or selling their information.

- **Thank you page:** Once your visitor has completed the form, you will have them as a lead, but before you let them go you can send them to a thank you page where you can offer them the opportunity to share your offer with their friends by including social sharing buttons.

- **Mobile Friendly:** You need to make sure your offer is easily visible and easy to complete on a mobile phone. This is incredibly important, as more and more people are purchasing from their mobiles. There is nothing more annoying for the user than if the site is hard to navigate from their mobile.

- Don't add external links to other sites. Be careful not to fall into the trap of wanting to make your site more interesting by adding lots of content and links to other external sites, as this will only detract from your main goals and you'll end up sending traffic away from your site.

Landing pages

Landing pages are incredibly effective if you want to promote specific offers for specific products to specific audiences. A landing page is a page that is designed to give information about an offer and then capture a lead with a form for your visitor to complete so that the visitor can download or claim that offer. Landing pages are highly effective in capturing leads because they are designed to be specific in their goal, which is to capture the contact information of your visitor.

The landing page should have a clear, uncluttered design and not have any links or navigation menus that could take your visitor away from the landing page. It should contain the following:

- A headline (The title of the offer)
- A description of the offer, clearly detailing the benefits to your visitor
- A compelling image of the offer
- A clear call-to-action. This can be in the form of an image or text.
- A form to capture contact information (The fewer fields that are required to be completed, the more leads you will receive.)
- A clear privacy policy on your website that makes it clear that you will not be spamming them or selling their information
- A thank you page leading them to another offer or social sharing

You can either ask your web developer to create landing pages or there are numerous tools available on the Internet where you can easily create one, for example: www.leadpages.net, www.unbounce.com, www.launcheffect.com, and www.instapage.com

SETTING UP AND CREATING YOUR EMAIL CAMPAIGN

Once you have created your lead capture system on your website, blog, or separate landing page and have your subscribers' permission to send them your email, you are going to need a really good email campaign to convert those leads into sales.

Email is still one of the most effective forms of converting leads into sales, and email is more powerful than ever. Not only is it cost effective but it also provides one of the most direct and personal lines of communication with your customer. Once subscribed, they have invited you into their inbox on a regular basis and producing valuable content for your subscribers will develop trust and deepen your relationship with your subscribers. Your email will also work hand in hand with your Instagram campaign. As you build your relationship with your followers on Instagram, they are more likely to deem your emails valuable and open them.

The first thing you need to do is set yourself up with a good email marketing provider and there are many you can choose from: www.aweber.com, www.constantcontact.com, and www.mailchimp.com to name a few. It's important to use a system where you have a confirmed opt-in. This is when the subscriber is sent an email to confirm their email address. This confirms that you are gaining consent and legally protects you. It also helps you to keep a clean list, and it protects you from sending emails to incorrect addresses. You can then automate your emails with an auto responder and send out emails automatically over time.

Your next task is to plan and create your email campaign. Here are a few tips for doing so:

- **Be clear about your goals:** You need to be absolutely clear from day one what you want to achieve through email. Are you using it to introduce a new product at some time? Are you launching an event? Whatever you do, make sure you know exactly what it is that you want to achieve.

- **Keep it simple and in line with your branding:** Make sure your email design ties in with your branding. Most email providers offer templates which you can add your own branding to, or you can get a designer to create a particular design. Keep it really simple. Sometimes if things are too fancy they become impersonal.

- **Send a regular newsletter:** Plan to send a regular newsletter email at least once a month and once a week if you can. You can also plan to send off information about offers which tie in with special holidays and occasions throughout the year or competitions or events that you may be planning.

- **Plan your topics:** You need to plan the topics you want to cover in each email, and this should tie in nicely with the plan for your blog articles. You then need to deliver high quality content which is tailor-made to fit with your subscribers' interests, and it needs to be so good that they are looking forward to the next email from you. If you are sending emails about offers then you need to show them clearly how these offers are going to benefit their lives.

- **Attention-grabbing titles:** This is where you need to get really creative. Your main goal here is to get your subscriber to open your email, and you need to create a headline that is going to make your subscriber curious and inquisitive and eager to open your mail. Questions work really well as titles, and you will often see your open rates increase. This is because people find questions intriguing and they feel like you are directly addressing them. Try and avoid the words that will trigger spam filters. Simply search Google for a list of these words to avoid.

- **Be authentic and true to your brand:** Write your emails in a style that your audience will grow to recognize, 'like,' and identify with your brand. Write so your subscriber feels like you are just writing to them. You need to establish yourself as a likeable expert for your subscribers. Try and create a personal relationship with them by addressing them by name and giving them a warm friendly introduction. Offering them the opportunity to connect with you and answer any of their questions by simply replying to your mail is a great way to create a connection and trust.

- **Keep it simple** Make sure your emails are simply constructed and straight to the point so you keep your subscribers' interest and get them quickly to the place you want them to go, like your blog or offer.

- **Include social sharing buttons:** Include all your social sharing icons and links in your mail.

- **Make them feel safe:** Make sure your subscribers are clear that their email will not be shared and that they can unsubscribe anytime.

- **Analyze your open rates:** Most email service providers include statistics in their packages so you can analyze open rates, bounce rates, click through rates, unsubscribers, and social sharing statistics. These results give you the opportunity to find out what is and what is not working.

CHAPTER ELEVEN

BLOG BLOG BLOG

THIS CHAPTER IS for anyone who does not have a blog. The word blog has been mentioned numerous times throughout the book and has become an essential part of any online business today.

WHAT IS A BLOG?

A blog (short for web log) is a term used to describe a website that provides an ongoing journal of individual news stories which are based around a certain subject or subjects (blog posts). Blogs have given people the power of the media. Anyone can now create a personal type of news that appeals to a high number of small niche audiences.

Bloggers simply complete a simple online form with a title and body and then post it. The blog post then appears at the top of the website as the most recent article. Over time, the posts build up to become a collection, which are then archived chronologically for easy reference. Each blog post can be a discussion with space for comments below the post where readers can leave comments and questions. This is where bloggers start to build relationships and a community with their readers and other bloggers who may have similar interests. Blogs were one of the earliest forms of social media, and they started growing in the late 1990s. The number of blogs has exploded in recent years, and they now underpin the majority of successful social media campaigns.

WHY BLOG FOR BUSINESS?

Blogging is one of the most beneficial tools that a business has to communicate its expertise and ideas to its prospects and customers and to engage with them. Businesses can share information about their business and about any subject that may be of interest to their niche. It is a fact that businesses with blogs benefit from an increase in the number of visitors to their website, increased leads, an increase in inbound links, and increased sales. Here are some of the reasons why and the benefits that come with blogging:

• **Underpins your whole social media campaign:** Your blog is the focus of all your social media efforts and the center of all your content marketing efforts. One of the main goals of any business today will be to get people to their blog to read their valuable and targeted content. Social media will be one of the main tools they can use to drive traffic to their blog.

• **Increased website traffic:** A well-optimized blog will increase your chances of being found in searches. Google loves unique, fresh content, and if this is created regularly, it will boost your traffic.

• **Builds brand awareness**: A blog offers a business the opportunity to build a community and awareness for their products or services. The more people who see your blog, the more people see your brand.

• **Provides valuable information for your niche:** Creating a blog gives your business a voice and provides your niche with valuable information in relation to the subjects they are interested in. This may include information about market trends, industry news, and insight into your products and services and what is behind them.

• **Thought leadership:** Sharing your expertise with valuable information will make you stand out as a thought leader in your particular field and help you build a professional online reputation.

• **Builds trust & creates warm leads:** When you are providing valuable content for your niche on a regular basis, answering their questions, and addressing their concerns, this in turn creates trust between you and your prospective customers. This trust leads to more leads and will result in sales. When your audience becomes regular readers of your blog, they become warm rather than cold leads. The ice has been broken, and they are halfway there in terms of buying your product.

• **You gain more knowledge:** While writing your blog you will be continually researching your subject, learning about new technology, products, and trends. In turn, this keeps you ahead of the game. In the eyes of your customers, it makes you an expert. As time goes by you become more and more knowledegable and can steer your business in line with market trends and keep your products and services up to the minute. You will also find that blogging is inspiring and your ideas will snowball. As you learn more, you will find more material to blog about.

• **Interaction and feedback:** When your blog has room for comments and discussion it will give you the opportunity to hear what people are saying, the questions they are asking, and insight into what they want out of your products. Feedback like this is invaluable to your business, and it also leads to more ideas for more blog posts. This kind of feedback also encourages a conversation, and you actually get the opportunity to communicate with prospective customers.

How to Create a Blog?

Creating your blog is incredibly straightforward. There are a number of free blogging platforms that are available. However, if you read the terms and conditions of most of these platforms you will find that at the end of the day you do not actually own the content and you will not have full control of your blog. You will have no control of the advertising displayed, you are unlikely to be able to include an email capture form, you will not be able to have you own domain name, and you will not be able to install plugins. With a free platform, your domain name will look something like http://mybusinessblog.theirblogplatformname.com. Overall, it is not going to look that professional.

The best and safest way of creating a blog and running with your own domain name is to create one with wordpress.org or you can use website creators like www.wix.com or www.squarespace.com. Both website creators offer blogs with their product, and you can add your own domain. Using any of these will give you full control over your site.

Wordpress.org is a free open source platform, which means it can be modified and customized by anyone. You can use custom themes or choose from hundreds of free themes and plugins. The wordpress.org blogging platform is free, but you will need to purchase a domain name and host your site on your own server. However, most hosting companies offer inexpensive monthly plans and a one-click installation solution. You will also need to make sure you backup your blog. You may very well find that this is included in your hosting package.

WHAT MAKES A SUCCESSFUL BLOG?

For those businesses that are doing it right, blogging can be hugely beneficial. The company will often see an increase of over 50% of website visitors and leads. However, many blogs also fail to make any positive difference to a business, so it is essential that before you waste time and resources you understand what you need to do to create a successful blog:

Set Goals and objectives

First of all, you will need to be clear about what your marketing goals are and set clear objectives for what you want to achieve from your blog.

Example Goal 1

Increase brand awareness through Facebook.

Objective:

Achieve X number of shares per month on Facebook.

Example Goal 2

Increase Traffic to website from blog.

Objective:

To achieve an increase of X traffic from blog.

Example Goal 3

Increase the number of leads for product A.

Objective:

To gain X number of new opt-ins per week.

Example Goal 4

To create interaction and engagement.

Objective: To have at least X number of comments on each blog post.

Example Goal 5

To become a thought leader in the industry.

Objective:

To write X number of guest posts per month/year.

Example Goal 6

To increase the ranking of your blog in Google and Bing.

Objective:

To achieve X number of backlinks from other websites in 6 months.

Create top content for your audience

Again it's all about your audience and what they want, what they are interested in, what makes them tick, and what problems they need solved. If you can identify these things then you are half way to finding the valuable content that is going to keep your audience interested and engaged. When you create your content it needs to be either inspiring, educational, informative, or entertaining. If you can create content that people really value, they are more likely to share your content, sign up for your updates, and come back looking for more. Creating content around your product or services is not going to provide enough interest to your readers and it is unlikely to get shared. Of course the occasional post is okay, but try and keep away from this unless you can tie it in to something which is of real value to your audience.

Create a content plan

Your content plan is the backbone to your blog. You will need to decide what topics you are going to build your blog around so that you can stay consistent. There may be certain keywords you want to target and need to incorporate into your content. Once you know your topics or subjects, you can decide which types of posts you are going to create. There are numerous types of blog posts you can use, such as tutorials, how to's , interviews, reviews, book reviews, advice, Q and A's, case studies, trend reports, and the latest news in your industry. Once you have decided on all this, you then write a schedule. If you have certain events that happen every year in your industry, make sure you include these in your plan.

Newsworthy posts

Make sure you are blogging about what's new in your industry. Keep an eye on trending topics related to your industry so you can create blog posts that are really up-to-date. You can do this by checking out what is trending on the social sites and also signing up for Google alerts, which will keep you up-to-date on new info related to your interests and queries.

Frequent and consistent blogging

It is proven that the more high quality content you produce, the more views your blog will get. You will need to post at least once a week, if not more. Google loves fresh content so the more posts you have, the more opportunities you have to be found.

Optimize your blog for searches

Look for keywords and phrases that people are looking for. There are tools available to do this, like word tracker, Google trends, and Google keyword planner. You can find out the amount of competition by typing a phrase into Google search and seeing how many results it brings up. In order to get found you will need to concentrate your efforts on low competition keywords and phrases, and the more specific your words and phrases are, the better. You can then create your content around your chosen keyword or phrase, as long as the content is highly relevant. When creating your blog post, make sure you put the word/

phrase in the page title, the header, and the body. If you put the phrase in your meta tag, it will be displayed in bold font in the search results, which will make it stand out even more.

Attention grabbing headline

To catch your readers' attention, you need a good headline. It should be a headline that will intrigue your audience enough to make them feel that they absolutely have to read this post. It needs to be simple and to the point, as well as contain valuable keywords. Here are some example headlines that really work:

How to ....
7 ways to successfully ....
Why you should do ..... to ....
Secrets that every ...... should know
The secret formula for success in ......
5 quick and easy ways to ....
What every serious ...... should know about......
7 things every ..... should avoid to ......

A great design

Your blog needs to be inviting, and although the content is what people are looking for, the blog still needs to be visually appealing and reflect your brand. If your blog is just text based, it's going to look cold and uninviting and lack interest, so you need to include compelling images to engage your audience. It is definitely a good idea to spend time researching different themes. Another thing to watch with your design is your side bar. Make sure you have only what is absolutely necessary so you do not pull your readers' attention away from the action you want them to take.

Formatting

You need to make it as easy as possible for your reader to read and digest your blog. If you format your blog with headings, bold subtitles, and bullet points, it will be much more enjoyable to read than one long paragraph.

Ask a question at the end of your post

Asking a question at the end of your post is likely to provoke discussion. People like to think their opinions matter, and it's a great way for your readers to interact and network with each other, too. Make sure you answer any questions your readers ask. There is nothing worse than seeing bloggers ignoring their readers.

Tags

Tags help people find your content within your blog and search engines. They also help group related posts together.

11 THINGS EVERY BLOG SHOULD HAVE

An incentive to join your opt-in

One of the main goals of your blog is to captures leads. The majority of your readers will probably only read one of your blog posts so it's really important to try and get them on your opt-in list so they will keep reading your blog. You will need to make sure you give them some kind of incentive to complete the email capture form, like a free report, free ebook, or simply email updates.

An engaging image

A blog needs at least one image to make it look interesting and inviting. Blogs without images are simply boring. You can use your own images, stock photos, or images from photo sharing sites like Flickr.

Clear call-to-actions

You need to make it very clear both within your text and outside your text what you want your readers to do. This could be anything from signing up for email updates, a free trial, a free offer, a request for a quote, or more information on a product.

Email capture form

You can either include a prominent form on your blog or install a pop-up mail capture form. If you do install a pop-up then make sure the reader has a good few seconds to read the heading and start reading the article before the form pops up. It is also a good practice to put at least three email sign-up forms on the page, one below the article, one in the footer, and one on the top beside the article or right above it.

About section

Your "about" section is the introduction to you and your blog. It's probably the most viewed page of any blog. People like to know who is writing the blog and feel acquainted with that person, so you need to get your personality over in this section. Make sure you include your name and a picture of yourself. This will help your readers make a personal connection with you. A video of yourself is also a great a way of getting your readers acquainted too. Above all, focus on how you are going to help your readers, what problems you are going to solve for them, and introduce some of the topics you are going to talk about. Remember, your blog is about your audience's needs and not yours.

Contact page

A simple contact form works best but also make it really easy for people to reach out to you. Make sure you include all your social sharing buttons and an email capture form.

Easy to search archives

If the content of your blog posts is interesting, then your readers are going to want to read more so you need to make the previous blog posts easily accessible. On many sites it really is incredibly difficult to find content, so you will need to get yourself a custom archive page. A search box at the top of your blog is a great idea for helping your readers find content.

Social sharing plug-ins

You need to include buttons or links to all the social networks where you have a presence. There are hundreds of plug-ins you can use to do this. Also make sure you have sharing buttons next to your articles as well.

RSS Feed

RSS (Rich Site Summary) is a format for delivering regularly changing content on the Internet. It saves you from checking the sites you are interested in for new content. Instead, it retrieves the content from sites you are interested in. Make sure you have the RSS feed and then have a clear call-to-action making it clear why they should subscribe to your feed. If you want to keep up-to-date with your favorite bloggers you can sign up to either My Yahoo, www.bloglines.com, or www.newsgator.com.

Comments section

Your blog needs a comment section which will encourage interaction and help you to build relationships with your readers. You can install Facebook comments easily with a WordPress plug-in. Disqus is another favorite comment provider.

A guest bloggers welcome page

Guest posting is becoming more and more important in the blogging community and making it obvious that you will accept guest posts is going to go a long way to building relationships with other bloggers. The benefits of having other people contributing to your blog are that you will have more valuable content on your site and more exposure if your guest blogger promotes their posts on their site. You may also gain from the opportunity to produce a guest post on their blog at a later date. Guest blogging is a top method of getting back links to your blog, which is essential for search engine optimization.

Privacy policy & terms of service pages
Make it clear your email readers are safe with you and you are not going to share their information with any other parties.

PROMOTING YOUR BLOG

If you want to run a successful blog, you cannot just rely on search to get it out into the blogosphere. You need to find other ways of promoting your content and getting found.

- **Promote on your social sites:** Posting your blog content on social sites is essential. You can connect your blog to Twitter and Facebook so your content is automatically shared. Or you can use Hootsuite or Tweetdec to share your content to multiple sites, which will save you time. When posting, use an image to grab your audience's attention and make sure you use popular hashtags for your topic which will open up more opportunities to being found by new people.
- **Guest blogging:** Guest blogging is a great way of gaining a larger following. It will also give your blog more exposure, credibility, and increase your inbound links, which is essential for SEO. Most bloggers allow guest bloggers to post their bio, including their social profiles and blog URL, on their site.
- **Social sharing buttons:** As mentioned previously, it is essential to have social sharing buttons next to your blog articles.
- **Comment on other blogs:** There is so much opportunity for you to promote yourself today with the number of blogs and social sites. If you comment on other peoples' blogs you can often leave a URL, but only if it is relevant to the article being

commented on and you are adding some value to the article.

- **Website and email:** If you have a website then try and point people to your blog. You can do this by adding visual links on your "about" page and other pages. Also make sure you have a link to your blog in your email and send an email to your current contacts telling them about your blog.

- **Create a Google Adwords campaign:** If you are serious about driving traffic to your site and generating leads and you have your blog set up to catch leads and subscribers, an Adwords campaign may kick start your traffic while you are waiting for your blog to get found naturally in search results. Getting quick results like this will also allow you to see if your blog design and format is working and whether any incentives you are offering are enough to generate subscribers and leads.

- **Submit your blog to Reddit and Stumbleupon:** Both of these websites allow their uses to rate web content. Reddit is a collection of webpages which have been submitted by its users. Stumbleupon is a collection of web pages that has been given the thumbs up. You can submit pages directly on its submit page or by installing the Firefox add-on or the Chrome extension. It is best not add too many of your own pages to Stumbleupon but make sure you add both the Reddit and Stumbleupon buttons to your blog so other people can.

THE ESSENTIAL WORDPRESS PLUGINS

One of the best things about WordPress for your blog is that it is easy to customize and you need little or no technical or design knowledge to create a great blog. There are a ton of plug-ins you can install to make your site even better, but there are so many it is difficult to choose which ones are really important. To help you, here are some plug-ins that are essential for your blog:

- **The Facebook comments plugin:** Installing Facebook comments into your blog can be tricky, but with this easy to use plugin you can easily administer and customize Facebook comments from your WordPress site. Another plugin, **Facebook comments SEO,** will insert a Facebook comment form, Open Graph tags, and insert all Facebook comments into your WordPress database for better search engine optimization. When it comes to spammers, Facebook with Open Graph is managing to weed out spammers and trolls with great effectiveness. Facebook allows you to login with Facebook, Yahoo, and Microsoft Live.

- **Disqus comment system:** The other popular comment system Disqus replaces your WordPress comment system with comments hosted and powered by Disqus. It features threaded comments and replies, notifications and replies by email, aggregated comments and social mentions, full spam filtering, and black-and-white lists. Disqus allows you to login with Facebook, Twitter, and Google.

- **Facebook Chat:** This is great if you want to chat with your visitors in real time. When installed, Facebook Chat will display on the bottom right. This is great for supplying support on your site.

- **Broken Link Checker:** This essential plugin scans your site and notifies you if it finds any broken links or missing images and then lets you replace the link with one that works.

- **RB Internal Links:** This plugin assists you with internal links and cuts the risk of error pages and broken links.

- **Social Sharing Plugins:** There are numerous social sharing plugins available for WordPress. **Flare** is a simple yet eye-catching sharing bar that you can customize depending on which buttons you want to display. It helps to get you followed or 'liked' and helps get your content shared via posts, pages, and media types. The other great feature Flare has is that you can display your Flare at the top, bottom, or right of your post content. When Flare is displayed on the left and right of your posts, it follows your visitors down the page and conveniently hides when not needed. Other social sharing plugins include: **Floating Social Media Icon, Social Stickers,** and **Shareaholic,** to name but a few.

- **All-In-One Schema Rich Snippets:** Rich snippets are markup tags that webmasters can put in their sites in order to tell Google what type of content they have on their site so that Google can better display it in search results. It is basically a short summary of your page. Rich snippets are very interactive, let you stand out from your competition, and help with your search engine ranking. Unless you are a techie then implementing them can be tricky. However, this plugin makes it really simple by giving you a meta box to fill in every time you create a new blog post.

- **Contact Form Plugins:** It is very important to make it easy for your visitors to contact you, and a form really does help with this. There are numerous plugins available for you to easily install, and here are a few: **Contact 7, Fast Secure Contact form, Contact form, and Contactme.**

- **Simple Pull Quote:** The Simple Pull Quote WordPpress plugin provides an easy way for you to insert and pull quotes into your blog posts. This is great for bringing attention to important pieces of information and adding interest to a post.

- **Backup Plugins:** Backing up your files and database is essential. It may be that your hosting service provides this, but there are very good plugins that do this: Vaultpress, BackWPup, Backup buddy, and Backup.

- **Related Posts Plugins:** Related post plugins help your visitors to stay on your site by analyzing the content on your site and pulling in similar articles from your site for them to read. One of the most popular ones is **nrelate related** content which is simple to install and activate. **WordPress related posts** is another one.

- **Search Everything Plugin:** This plugin increases the ability of the WordPress search, and you can configure it to search for anything you choose.

- **Google Analytics Plugin:** The Google Analytics plugin allows you to easily integrate Google Analytics using Google Analytics tracking code.

- **Google XML Sitemaps:** It is essential that the search engines can index your site and this plugin will generate a special XML sitemap.

- **SEO Friendly images:** This plugin automatically adds alt and title attributes to all your images, which helps to improve traffic from search engines.

- **Akismet (Comments and Spam):** The more traffic you receive, the more likely it is for you to receive spam and fake comments. Akismet checks your comments against Akismet web services to see if they look like spam or not and then lets you review it under your comments admin screen.

- **Social Author Bio:** Social Author Bio automatically adds an author box along with Gravatar and social icons on posts.

- **Thank Me Later:** This great little plugin automatically sends a thank you note by email to anyone who has commented on your blog. You can personalize your email and set up exactly when you want to send it, and you can set it up to only send it out once or as a chain of emails. This plugin is great for engaging people who comment on your blog, and you could use it to encourage people to join your opt-in.

MEASURING YOUR RESULTS

Measuring the success of your blog is crucial in order to steer your blog in the right direction so that your business can benefit from all the rewards a top blog can offer. Here are a number of ways you can measure your success:

Google Analytics

You can easily measure the number of social media shares, number of leads, subscribers, and comments on your blog. For more detailed information on your blog performance, setting up a Google Analytics account is essential and will offer you a wealth of detailed information so you can measure results, including the following:

- **The number of back links:** In the left side bar under **Standard Reports** you will find a section **Traffic Sources,** and then under **Social,** you will find **Trackbacks**. You will find here any web pages that have linked to any page of your site with the number of visits.

- **The number of visits:** Obviously this is one of the most important statistics, and you will be able to see easily how many visits you have and information about where your traffic is coming from.

- **Page views:** You will be able to see which pages are generating the most interest, and therefore, you will be able to plan more content similar to this.

- **Keywords:** You can keep track of your success with how your traffic is being generated by keywords. You will be able to see if your optimization for certain keywords are working and whether your blog is being found by keywords that you had not considered. When you identify which keywords are the most popular, you can try and work them into other blog posts.

- **Conversions:** In Google Analytics you will also be able to track conversions, which is an action on your site that is important to your business. This could be a download, sign up, or purchase. You will need to define your goals in analytics in order to track the conversion. You will be able to see conversion rates and also the value of conversions if you set a monetary value. There are detailed instructions available in Google Analytics on how to set this up, or you can employ a web developer or specialist to set this up.

CHAPTER TWELVE

THE ICING ON THE CAKE!

FOLLOWING ALL THE steps, instructions, and strategies is going to go a long way to making your campaign succeed, but what does it take to make you really good? If you have ever followed or are following certain brands on social media, you will probably have discovered that there are certain brands or businesses that stand out from the crowd. These are the brands and businesses that seem bigger than their products. These are the ones who usually have a sizeable and highly targeted audience, the best quality content, the greatest amount of interaction and engagement, and often post viral content. They literally have their audience hanging on their every word and get the highest open rates for their emails. They appear to understand their audience and relate to them by going out of their way by either helping them to achieve their dreams, calm their fears or confirm their suspicions, and offer them incredible value. It is obvious by the interaction that they have built a loving and respecting community, and you can be almost sure that all this is transferring to their balance sheets. These businesses are what I call 'The Social Media Superstars.' They are the game changers and they truly know how to leverage the power of social media to work for their business.

These 'Social Media Superstars' can often be compared to those party animals, the ones who always seem to be the most popular at any party and are more often than not surrounded by an audience of engaged and happy people having a great time. These people also always seem to be the most interesting, the most interested, the most charismatic, and the most engaged. They almost always tend to be good listeners as well. So how can you emulate this scenario, and what does it take to stand out from the crowd in Instagram marketing?

It's all about your audience and a few other things!

The reasons these individuals, businesses, and brands are good at social media marketing is not because they have particular powers. It's not by chance or coincidence. It's because they know that it's all about the audience and a few other things!

Of course your aim is to ultimately benefit your business, but in order to do this you need to make it all about your audience and what they want. If you give them what they want by either making their life better or easier in some way or solving a problem they may have, then you are going to build a valuable base of followers who trust you, open your emails, and are ready to go to the next step and buy your product. You will find that your followers will become ambassadors and advocates and will then be doing the work for you by sharing your content and promoting your brand in the most powerful way, word-of-mouth. To achieve this and stand out from the crowd, you need to go the extra mile by doing the following:

- Being fully committed and positive about your campaign and in it for the long term
- Totally believing in what you are offering. This could be your product, your service, or yourself, if you are a personal brand.
- Making it all about your audience, knowing exactly who they are, what makes them tick, what they need, and how to connect with them
- Putting your audience's needs above your own and demonstrating the rich content and service you provide
- Putting the relationship with your audience first, by listening to them, understanding them, and embracing conversation where you can
- Offering your audience incredible value with free information and advice
- Being authentic and true to your brand

So if there is one piece of insight I want to leave you with, it is this:

IT'S ALL ABOUT YOUR AUDIENCE and WHAT THEY WANT

I really hope you have enjoyed the book, that you have found it of great value, and that you will continue using it as your manual for your success on Instagram. The world of social media is continually changing, and it is my commitment to keep updating the books as and when these changes happen. If you would like to continue receiving these social media updates by email, please sign up at www.alexstearn.com

I would love your feedback about the book and would be very grateful if you could take just a moment to leave a review on Amazon at this link . By leaving a review, you can also enter the Prize draw for a Kindle Fire HD at this link and, of course, please feel free to contact me if you have any questions, at alex@alexstearn.com

I have also written a series covering all the major social media platforms including: Facebook, Google +, Pinterest, LinkedIn Tumblr, YouTube and Twitter. The content on social media is common to all books and therefore if you are planning be purchase more I would suggest purchasing the big book which includes the complete series Make Social Media Work for your Business is available on Amazon from $9.99 here.

Lastly, I have also set up a group on Instagram called 'Make Social Media Work for your Business.' The group was created for supporting each other in our social media efforts, for networking, and also as a place for finding out about the latest social media developments. You can join at this link: Join Now

I will also be continually posting helpful and inspirational tips on my Instagram page, and I look forward to connecting with you there or on any of your preferred social networks

Website: www.alexstearn.com
www.instagram.com/alexstearn
www.google.com/+alexstearn
www.facebook.com/alexandrastearn
www.twitter.com/alexstearncom
www.pinterest.com/alexstearn
www.alexstearn.tumblr.com
www.youtube.com/alexstearn
www.linkedin.com/in/alexstearn

The complete series in one book!

If you liked this book and wish to purchase any of the other books in the series I would suggest the most cost effective way of doing this is to purchase the big book that includes all the titles rather than the individual titles.
Make Social Media Work for your Business is available from $9.99

Make Social Media Work for your Business
The complete guide to marketing your business, generating new leads, finding new customers, and building your brand on Twitter, Pinterest, LinkedIn, Instagram, Google +, Tumblr, YouTube, Facebook, Foursquare,Vine and Snapchat.

Individual Books

Make Twitter Work for your Business

Make Instagram Work for your Business

Make Pinterest Work for your Business

Make Google + Work for your Business

Make YouTube Work for your Business

Make Tumblr Work for your Business

CPSIA information can be obtained at www.ICGtesting.com
Printed in the USA
LVOW10s0031101215

466180LV00028B/1017/P